The Godless Delusion

Joe Egan

THE GODLESS DELUSION

Dawkins and the Limits of Human Sight

PETER LANG

Oxford · Bern · Berlin · Bruxelles · Frankfurt am Main · New York · Wien

Bibliographic information published by Die Deutsche Bibliothek
Die Deutsche Bibliothek lists this publication in the Deutsche Nationalbibliogra-
fie; detailed bibliographic data is available on the Internet at <http://dnb.ddb.de>.

A catalogue record for this book is available from The British Library.

Library of Congress Cataloging-in-Publication Data:

Egan, Joe, 1954-
    The godless delusion : Dawkins and the limits of human sight / Joe
Egan.
        p. cm.
    Includes bibliographical references and index.
    ISBN 978-3-03911-899-1 (alk. paper)
    1. Apologetics. 2. God--Proof. 3. Religion and science. 4. Dawkins,
Richard, 1941- God delusion. 5. Atheism. 6. Religion--Controversial
literature. I. Title.
    BT1103.E35 2009
    211'.8--dc22
                            2009000504

Cover design: Mette Bundgaard, Peter Lang Ltd
ISBN 978-3-03911-899-1

© Peter Lang AG, International Academic Publishers, Bern 2009
Hochfeldstrasse 32, Postfach 746, CH-3000 Bern 9, Switzerland
info@peterlang.com, www.peterlang.com, www.peterlang.net

Printed in Germany

For
Simon and Andrew
and
Eoin, Niamh and Róisín

Contents

8

Introduction

The universe is a vast and awe-inspiring place. It is a place of wonder that never ceases to surprise those whose minds are open to its incredible beauty and to its immense complexity. That beauty and complexity have traditionally been traced by religious believers of every persuasion to a divine source, however that source is conceived and the originating act explained. In earlier eras of human history, a variety of stories, most notably in Western society the biblical creation story found in the book of Genesis, came to be written to express that conviction in mythological and religious terms. In the Christian vision, which builds on that Jewish understanding, the world in its entirety has been created by God, who has become fully manifest in Jesus Christ and who never ceases to watch over and guide all things providentially.

In more recent times, however, particularly since the nineteenth century when God's existence came to be explicitly denied in the name of atheism, those earlier approaches to the world's existence have been superseded, in the Western world particularly, by a scientific approach that purports to understand and explain everything in strictly rational terms. The two contrasting approaches provide a framework for Richard Dawkins's stance towards the world as articulated in *The God Delusion*, of which two editions have so far been published: London: Bantam Press, 2006; and London: Black Swan, 2007.

Dawkins begins his work by eliminating one by one the traditional arguments for God's existence, dismissing most of them as utterly unconvincing and absurd. Then, drawing on scientific probability, he proceeds to argue that the existence of God, though not scientifically disprovable as such, is so improbable that it can safely be regarded as a delusion. In the materialistic, atheistic scenario which he goes on to develop, he assigns a pivotal role to Charles Darwin's discovery of natural selection in 1859. That discovery was revolutionary, he argues, because it raised human consciousness to a level where the process of generating complexity out of simplicity could be explained in a purely natural way, without recourse to a supernatural designer. The gene, as the archetypal unit of life that is capable of making exact copies of itself, is central to that process. A somewhat analogous process takes place at the cultural level, where memes, which are also good at getting copies of themselves made, arise, spread within the human community and play a key role in shaping both our lives and the socio-cultural milieu in which we live.

Dawkins pulls no punches in detailing the evil that can be traced to religious belief, the fundamental problem with which is its irrationality, manifest by its capacity to hold onto beliefs for which there is no evidence. The result of this, he concludes, is that religion is a highly divisive force, fostering enmity, sustaining hatred and underpinning much of the fanaticism that brings so much destruction to the world. In sharp contrast, the scientific vision he champions is underpinned by evidence, which allows science to push against the limits of our puny understanding and to open the human mind to new vistas and liberating possibilities.

In light of the upbeat claims Dawkins makes for the sciences, it goes without saying that all readers of his work could genuinely expect to glean numerous insights that would open their minds and empower them to improve their lives. Theologians, in particular, could genuinely expect to learn much from this scientific incursion in the territory normally held as their preserve. The scientific rigour of his thought in exposing God as a delusion should, at the very least, alert them to the deficiencies in their own thinking, and thereby help them to improve it; or, in the unlikely event that his arguments were actually correct, lead them to pursue other, more fruitful interests instead.

That willingness to engage with those who raise objections to it has been a defining characteristic of Christian faith from earliest times. Within the New Testament itself, for example, believers are exhorted to be always 'ready to make your defence to anyone who demands from you an accounting for the hope that is in you' (1 Pet 3:15). Faithful to that exhortation and never shirking the challenging questions posed to them, Christian thinkers subsequently in every age of history responded to the philosophies and theories of the times as they arose, all the while seeking to deepen further their own understanding of the faith they cherished. As that understanding deepened, so theology came to develop in a manner captured succinctly by traditional definition of the discipline as 'faith seeking understanding'. Though ultimately rooted in faith, an extraordinary gift which in Christ underpins 'the assurance of things hoped for, the conviction of things not seen' (Heb 11:1), that assurance and conviction are far from being irrational and delusory sentiments. On the contrary, as has been well flagged from earliest times, they and the faith that upholds them are entirely reasonable, inherently rational acts.

It was with this basic stance that I took up *The God Delusion* towards the end of 2006, and this work is the fruit of my reflections on it. To develop those reflections, I also draw occasionally on some of Dawkins's other published work and on the work of his scientific contemporaries. It is my hope in bringing these reflections to publication that this work will complement several insightful critiques of Dawkins's work that have been published in the meantime.

The work itself is divided in two parts, each with three chapters. The focus in Part I is on a critique of *The God Delusion*. After an initial look at some contextual inaccuracies that arise in Dawkins's presentation of Christian belief, the first chapter questions his use of statistical probability, before going on to highlight a number of basic inadequacies in the ethical stance he adopts towards evil. Taking up the argument from there, attention in the second chapter is directed towards some key beliefs expressed by Dawkins in the course of the book, with a view to showing how they influence his conception of things so fundamentally that he even manages to bring off the far-from-inconsiderable achievement of calling not just God into question as a delusion but reality in its entirety into question as an illusion of some kind. In the third chapter, the critique is broadened to probe some of the ideological underpinnings of contemporary scientific methods and practice. In so doing, the attempt is made to highlight the flaws and inadequacies of these approaches and to show how the God question surfaces as a result.

Written from a faith perspective, the focus in Part II of the work shifts to explicating the stance of Christian faith towards some of the key underlying beliefs challenged by Dawkins in the course of his work, with the intention of showing how they actually provide a far sounder basis on which to ground scientific endeavours than the atheistic one he furnishes. The fourth chapter presents an overview of the theology of creation, viewing it as the handiwork of God who lovingly brought it into existence and who continues to sustain it, all the while working through natural processes that are not only open to the divine but can also be probed by the sciences. The question of freedom occupies centre stage in the fifth chapter, as the light of faith is brought to bear on the evil that plagues the world, with a view to showing how freedom is perfected in Jesus Christ and his redemptive acts. Then, in the sixth and final chapter, the attempt is made to show how all things come together and find their completion in a mystery that far exceeds our capacity to grasp and understand: the mystery of God's self-emptying love revealed in Jesus Christ which, in exposing us to his divine light, both reveals our blindness and heals our vision.

I am deeply indebted to all who helped me to bring this work to a conclusion. In the first place, I owe an enormous debt of gratitude to my family for their enduring love. My colleagues in the Society of African Missions have been a constant support, while my colleagues at the Milltown Institute of Theology and Philosophy have provided me with a stimulating intellectual environment in which to engage with some of the critical theological issues of today. Special thanks go to Michael McCabe, Jim Corkery and Kevin O'Gorman who read drafts of this work and whose insightful critiques shed light on many of the problems with which I grappled, thereby hopefully enabling me both to avoid falling into some of the pitfalls which I identified in the work of Dawkins and to start digging some fresh ones of my own.

JOE EGAN

PART I

Science and Pseudo-Science

Where is the one who is wise? Where is the scribe?
Where is the debater of this age?

1 CORINTHIANS 1:20

CHAPTER 1

Natural Selectivity

What this professor says is far more incredible that what we poor Christians believe.
— FRANÇOIS MAURIAC[1]

I have always thought it curious that, while scientists claim to eschew religion, it actually dominates their thoughts more than it does the clergy.
— FRED HOYLE[2]

The God-hypothesis will not be mocked without cost. But as the great mathematician and astronomer Laplace caustically put it, it is just of this hypothesis that the sciences (and technology) have no compelling need.... Until now, authentic atheism has been rare. Nor does it mock the God-hypothesis.
— GEORGE STEINER[3]

According to Dawkins, two alternative and mutually incompatible explanations of the world have been proposed: the hypothesis of ultimate design or the God hypothesis, on the one hand, that '*there exists a superhuman,*

---

1   François Mauriac, as quoted by Jacques Monod, *Chance and Necessity: An Essay on the Natural Philosophy of Modern Biology*, trans. Austryn Wainhouse (London: Collins, 1972) 131. A slightly different translation of the same is quoted by Joseph Ratzinger, *In the Beginning: A Catholic Understanding of the Story of Creation and the Fall*, trans. Boniface Ramsey (Edinburgh: T & T Clark, 1990) 24.

2   Fred Hoyle, as quoted by William J. O'Malley, *God: The Oldest Question* (Chicago: Loyola Press, 2000) 32.

3   George Steiner, *Grammars of Creation* (London: Faber and Faber, 2001) 279–280.

*supernatural intelligence who deliberately designed and created the universe
and everything in it, including us'* (31 [52])⁴; and, on the other hand, the
hypothesis of gradual evolution through natural selection that *'any creative
intelligence, of sufficient complexity to design anything, comes into existence
only as the end product of an extended process of gradual evolution'* (31 [52]).
In the course of his work, Dawkins investigates both these approaches
to life in the universe, delivering a devastating critique of the first and an
impassioned defence of the second.

  The God Delusion certainly provides food for thought to anyone
with an interest in religion. Written in a very engaging style, it outlines
what seems to be a compelling argument against religious belief from a
standpoint that rejects it as utterly nonsensical. By means of logical argument, ostensibly buttressed by scientific evidence, and combined with a
highly rhetorical style laced with ridicule, it furnishes numerous examples
in support of the argument that war, violence and abuses of every sort
are traceable to religious faith in God – an hypothesis for which there is
absolutely no evidence whatsoever to support.

  Notwithstanding its dismissal of theology as utter nonsense, there
is undoubtedly much in *The God Delusion* with which a theologian or,
indeed, any believer can concur; for it is undeniably true that there is no
shortage of contemporary examples of evil actions by religious people and
that abuse of any kind, done for whatever reason, religious or otherwise,
is truly evil. Yet, that basic agreement notwithstanding, for every point
on which one finds oneself in agreement with Dawkins, there are several
even more fundamental points of disagreement. To these we must now
turn, beginning with the need for contextual accuracy in evaluating any
position that purports to be reasonable.

---

4   As noted in the introduction, two editions of *The God Delusion* have so far been
     published. Since the pagination is different in each of these editions, references to
     both are included within brackets in the main text of this work: the first number
     given refers to the relevant page in the original edition of the work; the number
     within the square brackets refers to the relevant page in the second edition.

The Problem of Contextual Inaccuracy

In the preface to *The God Delusion*, immediately after quoting an opponent of Darwinism, Dawkins notes how statements of his own have been deliberately taken out of context by those who oppose his views: 'I hope the fact that I have stated as much will be noted, since the same courtesy has not been extended to me in numerous creationist quotations of my works, deliberately and misleadingly taken out of context' (5 [27–28]). Given this concern for contextual accuracy, it is strange that it is manifestly lacking in his own treatment of theological assertions that go right to the very heart of Christian belief. In critiquing the Nicene Creed, for example, Dawkins zeroes in on the denial by a group of believers at the time that 'Jesus was *consubstantial* (i.e. of the same substance or essence) with God' (33 [54]). He goes on to ask concerning this expression: 'What on earth could that possibly mean, you are probably asking? Substance? What "substance"? What exactly do you mean by "essence"? "Very little" seems the only reasonable reply' (33 [54]). An examination of the history of the councils of the early Church, at which the creed was formulated (Nicaea in 325 and Constantinople I in 381), would have provided a very clear answer to what the terms 'substance', 'consubstantial' and 'essence' meant in the context of the time and how they were to be correctly understood.[5] In place of the effort required for such an exercise, however, Dawkins simply resorts to sarcasm and misrepresentation, implying the term 'substance' is to be understood in the identical way it is used in contemporary English, to speak of material objects of one kind or another, and equating 'essence' with 'very little'. In thus caricaturing the creedal statement, he distorts its meaning entirely. The discourtesy he attributes to others, of 'deliberately and misleadingly' taking statements out of context, is no less operative in his own writing.

---

5   Tarmo Toom furnishes a brief explanation of the key terms in early Christian theology in his work, *Classical Trinitarian Theology: A Textbook* (New York and London: T & T Clark, 2007) 36–43.

Context too has no relevance for Dawkins in his treatment of the
medieval proofs for the existence of God, which fare little better under his
scornful disdain. Though he does not quote Thomas Aquinas directly as
he summarises and dismisses his 'proofs' as worthless, he makes no effort
whatever to contextualise them before thus dismissing them. Readers are
left in the dark that Thomas, in putting forward the various arguments,
was drawing on the knowledge available to him at the time, particularly
the philosophy of Aristotle, which he modified decisively in the light of
Christian revelation to make a huge contribution to human learning and
to demonstrate clearly the rationality of Christian faith. For Thomas, God
is 'the One who is', the act of pure existence revealed as such to Moses in
the incident of the burning bush at the time of the Exodus – 'I am who I
am' (Ex 3:14).[6] Removed from that context where faith and philosophy
intersect, his arguments lose much of their cogency and power and are
easily subject to caricature. Within that context, however, the arguments
from limited acts of existence – motion, efficient causality, contingency,
and necessity – to the unlimited act of existence, whose name is 'I am
who I am', shows that revealed faith can be expressed perfectly reasonably
in philosophical categories.[7]

Dawkins's interpretation of the Biblical passages displays no more
sensitivity to context than the aforementioned examples. Though he
deems it 'a commonplace that good historians don't judge statements
from past times by the standards of their own' (266 [302]) and though
he seems to acknowledge that biblical history and literature – as opposed

6   See Fergus Kerr, *After Aquinas: Versions of Thomism* (Malden, MA, and Oxford,
     U.K.: Blackwell Publishing, 2002) 73–96, esp. 80–85.
7   For critiques of the position adopted by Dawkins here, see Thomas Crean, *A
     Catholic Replies to Professor Dawkins* (Oxford: Family Publications, 2007) 35–49;
     Nicholas Lash, 'Where Does *The God Delusion* Come from?' *New Blackfriars*
     88/1017 (September 2007) 507–521, at 508–509; and Nicholas Lash, *Theology for
     Pilgrims* (London: Darton, Longman & Todd, 2008) 3–18, at 4. See also Gerald
     A. McCool, *From Unity to Pluralism: The Internal Evolution of Thomism* (New
     York: Fordham University Press, 1989) 184; and Jean-Pierre Torrell, *Saint Thomas
     Aquinas*, Vol. 2, *Spiritual Master*, trans. Robert Royal (Washington, D.C.: The
     Catholic University of America Press, 2003) 40–49.

to theology – may actually be subjects worthy of study (see 57 [80]), his own approach to biblical stories is characterised by a notable lack of input from the aforementioned disciplines. For example, his treatment of Genesis 22:1–19, the 'morally obnoxious ... story of Abraham setting out to barbecue Isaac' (251 [284]), provides a good illustration of his method of placing religious stories in a very different context to the ones in which they originated: 'By the standards of modern morality, this disgraceful story is an example simultaneously of child abuse, bullying in two asymmetrical power relationships, and the first recorded use of the Nuremberg defence: "I was only obeying orders"' (242 [275]). In sharp contrast, he deems Adolf Hitler – the individual whose totalitarian regime actually eliminated huge numbers of people, literally barbecuing many of them in the process, and whose followers stood condemned at the Nuremberg trials – to be fairly benign by the standards of times past: 'Hitler seems especially evil only by the more benign standards of our time' (269 [305]).[8]

Dismissive comments about matters of religious faith and its content would have far greater credence and carry much more weight if reported accurately and with due attention to the context in which they originated. On the basis of the above analysis, however, it is clear that neither the content of faith, what Christians actually believe, nor the historical context in which it arose and the various historically conditioned means by which it has been articulated down though the ages, matter to any extent for Dawkins. Indeed, he considers all of these issues to be utterly tiresome and irrelevant – and no doubt the above remarks tiresome and irrelevant too – for since God is but a delusion, faith itself can only be delusive too and all attempts to give coherent conceptual expression to it are simply ludicrous in the extreme.

---

8   For a very different judgement on the 'ice cold reasoning' of Hitler, see Hannah Arendt, *The Origins of Totalitarianism* (New York: Schocken Books, 2004 [1948]) esp. 607–608. For more examples of how Dawkins misreads the Scriptures, see Alister McGrath, with Joanna Collicutt McGrath, *The Dawkins Delusion: Atheist Fundamentalism and the Denial of the Divine* (London: SPCK, 2007) 53–59; and Crean, *A Catholic Replies to Professor Dawkins*, 118–136.

At this point, it is necessary to take a closer look at the reason for Dawkins's utter certainty in relation to God and all things religious. To address those issues, we need to consider his approach to statistical probability.

Circular Argumentation

From the standpoint of Christian faith, miracles as divine interventions in nature and in history are far from routine occurrences. As instances of divine power, communicating the divine intentions and will, they occur relatively infrequently and in a manner intimately associated with faith in particular and with the life of the Church as a whole. Dawkins, therefore, is perfectly correct in observing that from a scientific standpoint 'miracles are events that are extremely improbable' (373 [419]).

As shown in the opening section, however, Dawkins's interest goes far beyond the purely miraculous as such, for he is intent in demonstrating not merely that God does not intervene in nature but that God does not exist at all. Statistical probability is the key to his method of demonstrating that very thesis, allowing him to conclude that 'the argument from improbability, properly deployed, comes close to proving that God does *not* exist' (113 [137]). In thus arguing, however, Dawkins leaves himself open to the charge of employing circular argumentation that predetermines the answers to the very questions he asks.[9] In relation to his overall approach, it is important to remember that the scientific elaboration of the 'laws of nature' cannot be equated with complete and exhaustive descriptions of the natural processes they purport to codify and explain. As Wolfhart Pannenberg observes, 'they are only approximations, although they may be more than sufficiently precise for

9   See McGrath, *The Dawkins Delusion*, 31.

most practical purposes'.[10] With reference to the biological sphere itself, for example, Dawkins indicates that 'what natural selection favours is rules of thumb ... Rules of thumb, by their nature, sometimes misfire' (220 [252]). Though it is possible with the tools of mathematics to be more precise in the physical realm, even there complete exactitude, however desirable, is not finally achievable in everyday conditions. Newton's laws, for example, approximate very accurately to the conditions of everyday life here on earth, but as Einstein at the cosmic level and quantum physicists at the atomic and sub-atomic levels have famously shown, when we move beyond the realm of everyday events they break down completely, so that more refined 'physical laws' (366 [411]) are necessary to do justice to those levels of physical reality. Thus, for example, applying the laws of Newtonian physics to the behaviour of sub-atomic particles is a recipe for wildly inaccurate and misleading results.[11]

The relevance of this for our concerns here centres on the fact that while statistical probability furnishes us with purely 'natural' laws, yet Dawkins – in considering whether *there exists a superhuman, supernatural intelligence who deliberately designed and created the universe and everything in it, including us* (31 [52]) – insists on applying those laws to a level that by his own definition is 'supernatural'. A basic problem surfaces immediately in relation to this approach, centred on the term 'supernatural'. It is clear from his use of the term that Dawkins understands 'supernatural' merely to mean a 'supersized' version of what is natural; in other words, the 'supernatural' can simply be considered as an 'ultra-sized' aspect or dimension or variation of the natural, entirely

---

10   Wolfhart Pannenberg, *Toward a Theology of Nature: Essays on Science and Faith*, ed. Ted Peters (Louisville, Kentucky: Westminster/John Knox Press, 1993) 36. See also Michael Polanyi, *Personal Knowledge: Towards a Post-Critical Philosophy* (London, Melbourne and Henley: Routledge and Kegan Paul 1973 [1958]) 18–20.

11   For discussions on the laws of nature, see Alister McGrath, *A Scientific Theology*, Vol. I, *Nature* (Edinburgh: T & T Clark, 2001) 225–232; and Paul Davies, *The Goldilocks Enigma: Why Is the Universe Just Right for Life?* (London and New York: Allen Lane, 2006) 8–13, 266–272.

circumscribed by it and fully defined by purely natural laws.[12] Such an understanding is far removed from the Christian understanding of the supernatural as wholly transcending the natural order and not simply comprising a part or, indeed, even the whole of it. In these terms, God is not an entity capable of being situated alongside other entities or of being measured and evaluated scientifically in the way natural entities are. On the contrary, as Terry Eagleton observes, God is 'the condition of possibility of any entity whatsoever, including ourselves. He is the answer to why there is something rather than nothing. God and the universe do not add up to two, any more than my envy and my left foot constitute a pair of objects'.[13] In light of these observations, it is patently obvious that Dawkins is setting out to undertake the task he has set himself with tools that are wholly incapable of completing it. Just as the rigid application of Newtonian 'laws' to every sphere of physics is folly, no less so is the attempt to apply 'statistical probability' rigidly to a realm that actually far transcends it. The problem emerges clearly in *The God Delusion*, though the underlying difficulty is ignored and the answer derived is presented as completely scientific and authoritative.

In the course of developing his argument for evolution, which he takes as scientifically demonstrable and evident, Dawkins spells out his basic premise: that 'entities that are complex enough to be intelligent are products of an evolutionary process. No matter how god-like they may seem when we encounter them, they didn't start that way' (73 [98]). A few sentences later he declares: 'The laws of probability *forbid* all notions of their spontaneously appearing without simpler antecedents' (73 [98–99];

12   This is but a contemporary variation of the God of seventeenth-century deism. See, for example, Hans Küng, *The Beginning of All Things: Science and Religion*, trans. John Bowden (Grand Rapids, Michigan, and Cambridge, U.K.: Eerdmans, 2007) 105–108; and Corey S. Powell, *God in the Equation: How Einstein Transformed Religion* (New York, London, Toronto, Sydney: Free Press, 2002) 11.

13   Terry Eagleton, 'Lunging, Flailing, Mispunching', *London Review of Books* (19 October, 2006); accessed at http://www.lrb.co.uk/v28/n20/eag101_.html 1–6, at 2 (19 July, 2008). See also Lash, 'Where Does *The God Delusion* Come from?' 509–511; Lash, *Theology for Pilgrims*, 5–6; and John Cornwell, *Darwin's Angel: A Seraphic Response to* The God Delusion (London: Profile Books, 2007) 61.

emphasis added).[14] It is immediately clear from this statement that the odds of a favourable answer to the theist position are negligible in the extreme. For, if it is the case that the 'laws of probability' actually 'forbid' complex entities to appear spontaneously 'without simpler antecedents', it means that probability theory is utterly incapable of investigating impartially and objectively the very scenario where that is precisely the issue in question. If 'the laws of probability' that Dawkins employs to address the question of the existence of a transcendent God (who initiates evolution without being part of it) actually 'forbid' the very scenario they are required to investigate, then the answer to the God Hypothesis is predetermined as negative, even before the investigation begins. Just as the 'laws' of Newtonian physics 'forbid' atomic and sub-atomic particles to behave in ways that scientists now tell us they do – for that world lies far beyond the parameters within which Newtonian laws are capable of functioning with any degree of accuracy – so the very application of probability laws to a question that by definition lies beyond their scope means the answer to God's existence is likely to deliver a wildly inaccurate and far from scientific result.

The approach adopted by Dawkins leaves the interpreter caught in a vicious circle involving the method employed and the data considered. On the side of the method, the laws of statistical probability, which he employs, forbid complex intelligible entities to appear in the absence of simpler antecedent ones, so that the question of a highly complex divine designer without antecedent really makes no sense and, strictly speaking, ought to be excluded forthwith.[15] On the side of the data, the evidence he finds for evolution is so overwhelming and for a designer of any sort so negligible that the existence of the latter is highly improbable even to begin with: '... there is no evidence to favour the God Hypothesis' (59 [83]). Thus, on the basis of non-existent positive data (for if God is

14 Keith Ward disputes this assertion; see his *Why There Almost Certainly Is a God: Doubting Dawkins* (Oxford: Lion, 2008) 47.

15 On the complexity of God, see, for example, 148–151 [177–180]. For a response that highlights the simplicity of God, see Ward, *Why There Almost Certainly Is a God*, 48–50.

non-existent, then genuinely favourable evidence to the contrary cannot surely be available) and by a method of investigation that precludes any favourable evidence even if it did exist (for the laws of statistical probability forbid anything other than that complex entities emerge from simpler ones), Dawkins, without a trace of irony but with impeccable logic delivers the blindingly obvious and far from scientific verdict furnished by his own presuppositions and his wholly circular process of argumentation:

> The whole argument turns on the familiar question 'Who made God?' ... A designer God cannot be used to explain organized complexity because any God capable of designing anything would have to be complex enough to demand the same kind of explanation in his own right. God presents an infinite regress from which he cannot help us to escape. This argument ... demonstrates that God, though not technically disprovable, is very very improbable indeed (109 [136]).[16]

A major difficulty confronting Dawkins' approach begins to appear at this point, for in simply taking material reality as a given and sidestepping the problem of an infinite evolutionary regress, he still has to come up with a credible explanation that accounts for the origin of life. How credible is the explanation he furnishes?

Giving Credence to an Old Adage

In considering the origin of life, involving the transition from inanimate matter to living creatures, Dawkins concedes that there does exist a major gap in the evolutionary story. His solution to this problem involves three distinct but inter-related issues: a vast number of planetary opportunities; an 'initial stroke of luck ... sheer luck, anthropically justified' (140 [168]);

---

16   Alternatively, the question can be framed: 'who designed the designer'? (See 158 [188]).

and the multiverse hypothesis. First of all, the vast number of planetary opportunities, arising from statistically informed science, allows the possibility of life arising naturally and spontaneously on a billion planets in the universe while ruling out a divine creator (see 138–139 [166–167]). Secondly, though the luck involved in bridging the gap marked by the origin of life is obviously enormous – 'near-impossible' (374 [419]), he concedes – the 'anthropic principle' grants that luck decisively and justifies it, because life on Earth happened and we exist (see 137 [165] and 140 [168]). And, finally, a genuinely simple solution to the 'anthropic principle' itself is provided by the multiverse hypothesis – that not just one, but many universes exist.

Though Dawkins is clearly satisfied with the elegant simplicity of this approach to the origin of life, it does leave a couple of rather large questions unanswered. For instance, in relation to the third issue above, is it possible to reach any conclusion on the probable number of universes in the multiverse? Unless the laws of physics explicitly restrict the number of universes to a few – which, interestingly enough, would have the effect of highlighting the uniqueness of this universe and of bringing to the fore once more the question of the underlying reason for that uniqueness – or unless the 'by-laws' operative in each of those universes distort the statistical probability in some way or other, then, presumably the same gigantic odds that apply to the emergence of life in this universe apply also to the number of universes suitable for life in the multiverse. Given, as we shall see, that the multiverse hypothesis seems to imply an infinite number of universes, it seems clear that this approach really offers no solution to the regress that it identifies as a problem; a problem from which, as we shall see, there is no way of escape – apart, that is, from the Creator God who utterly transcends this world.[17]

A second issue of concern to those unfamiliar with statistical probability centres on the amount of luck involved to allow the above scenario to work. Even if we grant that 'luck' is not synonymous with 'chance' – a

17   It is worth noting here the contention of physicist Paul Davies that 'many scientists hate the multiverse idea'. See Davies, *The Goldilocks Enigma*, 194–196; also Ward, *Why There Almost Certainly Is a God*, 54–56.

term Dawkins again and again rejects as inappropriate on the basis that 'the greater the statistical improbability, the less plausible is chance as a solution' (119 [145]) – we are still left with an event that is enormously improbable. Dawkins concedes as much when he acknowledges that the bridging of this major gap in the evolutionary story involves 'sheer luck' (140 [168]) and that 'maybe a few later gaps in the evolutionary story also need major infusions of luck, with anthropic justification' (141 [169]).[18] The question thus arises for the average theological mindset as to how that 'sheer luck' relates to the 'sheer cliff' (121 [147]) of 'Mount Improbable' that proved to be completely insurmountable only a few pages earlier in *The God Delusion* and that legitimated Dawkins in his confident dismissal of the notion of God – the 'ultimate Boeing 747' – as absurd: 'The absurd notion that such complexity could spontaneously self-assemble is symbolized by leaping from the foot of the cliff to the top in one bound. Evolution, by contrast, goes around the back of the mountain and creeps up the gentle slope to the summit: easy!' (122 [147]). Even leaping from the foot of the cliff to the top in one bound, however, is easy too – childishly easy, in fact – if the 'sheer cliff' arising in the face of religious questions is allowed to metamorphose into 'sheer luck' in matters biological, thereby lending credence to that old adage, 'lies, damned lies and statistics'! Funnily enough, that suggestion is practically identical with the charge Dawkins levels at theologians and believers in their defence of a supernatural deity.

The question of truth is a central plank in the highly sharp and sustained critique of religious belief that Dawkins presents in *The God Delusion*, as he argues that believers and theologians are well capable of bending the truth to suit their own ends, in the conviction that the human sense of right and wrong is intrinsically connected with the existence of a supernatural deity. Convinced that 'people of a theological bent are often chronically incapable of distinguishing what it true from what they'd

---

18   Dawkins alerts us to other 'one-off events' in the evolutionary story that are of the same order of improbability as the origin of life: the origin of the eucaryotic cell and the origin of consciousness. These he also justifies by appeal to the anthropic principle (see 140–141 [168–169]).

like to be true', Dawkins goes on to argue that for more sophisticated believers in some kind of supernatural intelligence, 'it is childishly easy to overcome the problem of evil. Simply postulate a nasty god – such as the one who stalks every page of the Old Testament' (108 [135]). There is, it has to be admitted, no shortage of detail in the evidence he marshals in support of his claims that religious belief fosters fanaticism and that it motivates and leads its adherents to undertake evil actions with disastrous consequences for everyone. Several other issues arise from his analysis, however, to the investigation of which we must now turn.

Religion and the Problem of Evil

Dawkins credits theologians with the uncanny ability to spot gaps in scientific knowledge and to fill every gap they spot with a supernatural deity. 'If an apparent gap is found', he states, 'it is *assumed* that God, by default, must fill it' (125 [151]; see also 128 [154]). Intriguingly enough, there are a number of tantalising gaps, badly in need of filling, in his own work. One such gap, a huge one, centres on the problem of evil, its nature and its source. That evil is a fact in the world is readily apparent from even a cursory reading of *The God Delusion*. On the basis of the approach found therein, however, how is the problem of evil to be addressed and ultimately overcome?

    In answer to that question, a fundamental point to be made is that since Dawkins rules out the existence of supernatural beings of any sort – good, bad or indifferent – then, it is patently obvious that the 'child-ishly easy' solution of postulating a 'nasty god' as its origin and source has to be excluded. Non-existent deities cannot be held responsible for evil and the blame for it cannot be pinned on them. Evil, in this perspective, can finally have no spiritual reference; it must be purely categorical and natural, originating and terminating solely in the material realm, since no spiritual realm exists. Though Dawkins does not directly address in the book the issue of what constitutes evil or wherein its source lies, the answer that suggests itself on the basis of the material he furnishes is along the following lines: a consequential but highly virulent by-product of natural events and human actions arising principally from unjustified religious beliefs. There are at least three levels involved in this approach to the question: a neutral moral stance towards the natural order of things; an emphasis on the consequences of an action or event as determinative of its moral status; and a focus on religion as highly virulent and destructive because of its rejection of the need for supporting evidence in the realm of belief.

At the first level, it is important to note the neutral moral stance adopted by Dawkins towards nature and its processes. In his presentation, nature itself is without design or purpose and natural processes are morally neutral and indifferent, neither good nor bad in themselves.[19] As he carefully explains, selfishness in the genetic order is not to be equated with selfishness in the moral realm; on the contrary, it is merely the gene's method of ensuring another generation of exact replicas of itself (see 215 [246–247]). Hence, there is nothing inherently 'good' or 'evil' in natural processes that are found in the world – even the most catastrophic and destructive of them, earthquakes, volcanic eruptions, tsunamis and so forth – for neither design nor purpose are at work in their occurrence.

If evil in the world cannot be blamed on a deity and it does not inhere in the natural order as such, then, it must be of human origin. Indeed, Dawkins implies as much when he affirms that 'cruel and evil people can be found in every century and of every persuasion' (312 [351]). As to how 'cruel and evil' individuals can be distinguished from compassionate and good ones at this second level, Dawkins leaves us in no doubt that it is by the consequences of their actions that such a judgement can be delivered. Describing himself as a consequentialist in moral terms (see 301 [340]), he adopts a position that stands over against the absolutism of those who adhere rigidly to moral absolutes of right and wrong. Consequentalists,

19   For further references, see Richard Dawkins, *River out of Eden: A Darwinian View of Life* (London: Phoenix, 1995) 133. See also Alister McGrath, *Dawkins' God: Genes, Memes, and the Meaning of Life* (Malden, MA, and Oxford: Blackwell Publishing, 2005) 49–50.

he explains, adopt a far more pragmatic stance, holding that there is no absolute foundation for moral choices and that 'the morality of an action should be judged by its consequences' (232 [266]). However, the atheist's personal decision to follow particular moral precepts that are without absolute foundation is not a recipe for moral laxity; it is no more a case of 'morality flying by the seat of its pants' (238 [269]) than is the decision of religious believers to pick and choose among the moral precepts they find in their Scriptures – to take the ones that appeal to them while rejecting as mere allegories those moral precepts which they now find objectionable in the Old Testament.

The third and, clearly for Dawkins, most important level to keep in mind in attempting to come to grips with evil is religion itself. Though he is careful not to single out religion as 'the root of *all* evil' – 'for no one thing is the root of all anything' (1 [23]) – and though he disavows responsibility for the title implying that it is of the Channel Four TV programme which he presented, Dawkins leaves the readers of *The God Delusion* in no doubt that religion is certainly a huge contributory factor, if not *the* determining one, in evildoing. Employing the term 'viruses' as 'a metaphor for religions' (186 [216]), he makes quite clear that he considers faith's inherent absolutism to be extremely dangerous, for it denigrates rational thought, turns ignorance into virtue and provides an environment where extremism and fanaticism can prosper: 'Faith is an evil precisely because it requires no justification and brooks no argument' (308 [347]). As we have already seen, his blunt conclusion is that the basic problem is not religious extremism, as though religion in its moderate, less extreme, forms is good; on the contrary, the fundamental problem is with religion itself, which even in moderate form is 'an open invitation to extremism' (306 [346]).

A fundamental problem with this whole approach is that Dawkins, in order to defend his thesis, is obliged to seek a religious angle, however obscure and however distorting of the evidence, to every situation in which evil occurs with the aim of identifying religion as the real culprit in the situation. His treatment of the actual tsunami that occurred in the Indian Ocean in 2004, leaving immense destruction and misery in its wake, is a case in point. In briefly considering that catastrophe, Dawkins ignores level one above (the event itself) and level two (human culpability for inept or, possibly even, corrupt administrative and political decisions that might have contributed to the loss of life in the catastrophe) to zero in immediately on level three (the religious dimension). His ire and ridicule are directed not at bad planning or incompetent administration or political corruption or anything else that served to exacerbate the loss of life, but rather at the interpretation of the event provided by some 'Asian holy men' in its aftermath. In highlighting their folly in blaming the tsunami 'not on a plate tectonic shift but on human sins, ranging from drinking and dancing in bars to breaking some footling Sabbath rule', he ridicules their whole education that 'has led them to view natural disasters as bound up with human affairs, paybacks for human misdemeanours rather than anything so impersonal as plate tectonics' (238 [270]). Though he stops short of blaming them for the catastrophic fallout to the event in the first place, that omission might be considered merely an oversight on his part, given the lengths to which he goes to in establishing links between religion and violent evil in other instances.

By contrast with religious faith, which inspires such fanaticism in its adherents that civilisation itself is endangered, Dawkins asks rhetorically, 'why would anyone go to war for the sake of an *absence* of belief?' (278 [316]). Well, one reason that springs to mind is in defence of a passionately held conviction, which could easily be atheistic rather than religious, that a fundamental value is under threat and that the only way of defending it is by recourse to violence. An 'absence of belief' should not simply be identified with a 'lack of conviction' and even atheists, we can safely presume after the examples furnished us by Stalin and Chairman Mao and Pol Pot in the course of the twentieth century, are not unwilling to fight and eliminate their opponents while defending and upholding their own passionately held convictions.[20] Yet the issues raised by Dawkins's question are far more complex than this, as quickly becomes apparent when we come to consider his treatment of the evil carried out under the totalitarian regimes of the twentieth century.

---

20   See McGrath, *The Dawkins Delusion*, 32, 46–49.

The Unravelling of the Moral Argument

Dawkins's treatment of Hitler and Stalin is particularly interesting, because the thrust of his argument is to shift as much of the blame as possible for their evil deeds onto religion, while overlooking atheism's notorious track record in violence and absolving it entirely of guilt.[21] Though this scenario is quite neat in one respect, the argument begins to unravel when he tries to convince us not only that 'Hitler's ideas and intentions were not self-evidently more evil than those of Caligula' (272 [308]), but that the critical difference between the two of them was that 'Hitler had twentieth-century weapons, and twentieth-century communications technology at his disposal' (272 [308–309]). That very admission is extremely significant, however, for in alerting us to the part played by technology in the destruction unleashed by Hitler, it also implicates those who provided him with the weaponry that rendered his evil intent far more destructive than that of Caligula. In so doing, it blows apart the very neat and tidy distinction Dawkins constructs between atheistic, wholly objective, evidence-based science, on the one side, and the mind-corrupting 'virus' that is religious faith, on the other: a distinction that would have us believe that the former in the absence of belief is wholly benevolent in its outcomes, while the latter precisely because of its belief is wholly evil in its; a bipolar vision that considers atheistic science to be wholly neutral and objective, praiseworthy and pure, in its rationality, even when furnishing tyrants with weapons of mass destruction, while arguing that when the tyrants use them for evil and destructive ends, they do so for religious reasons; in short, a 'black and white' argument that implies the 'good' atheistic scientists merely do the research and develop the technology for the benefit of humanity as a whole, but only the 'bad' religious believers utilise the technology to do the actual killing. Not only

---

21   In sharp contrast, he finds that the Christian faith of the great artists Raphael and Michelangelo 'is almost incidental' (86 [111]).

is this type of argument quite bizarre, but it actually completely distorts the historical evidence, which George Steiner describes as follows.

> Nineteenth-century liberalism and scientific positivism regarded as self-evident the expectation that the spread of schooling, of scientific-technological knowledge and yield, of free travel and contact among communities would bring with them a steady improvement in civility, in political tolerance, in the mores of private and public business. Each of these axioms of reasoned hope has been proved false. It is not only that education has shown itself incapable of making sensibility and cognition resistant to murderous unreason. Far more disturbingly, the evidence is that refined intellectuality, artistic virtuosity and appreciation, scientific eminence will collaborate actively with totalitarian demands or, at best, remain indifferent to surrounding sadism.[22]

As in other instances already considered above, Dawkins leaves himself open to the charge of manipulating the evidence to fit his theories rather than vice versa.

In terms of the moral dimension of the issue, and strictly from the moral standpoint Dawkins himself advocates, even a consequentialist would surely agree that for a perfectly rational person, in full possession of all his faculties, to give lethal technology to a highly imbalanced person is both dangerous and immoral; indeed, that the guilt of the perfectly clear thinking individual who does such a deed is far greater than that of the deranged individual, in the event of evil actions being carried out by the latter and destructive consequences ensuing. In parallel fashion, surely those clear-headed, atheistic scientists who furnish religiously motivated political and military leaders with weapons of mass destruction – biological, chemical and nuclear – are not unaware of the potentially lethal consequences of their actions? Indeed, is not the guilt of those scientists, with their raised consciousness and capacity for objective thinking, all the greater for the devastating consequences that ensue, when their political masters – infected with the most dangerous mind 'virus' of all, religious

22   Steiner, *Grammars of Creation*, 3–4. See also Tina Beattie, *The New Atheists: The Twilight of Reason and the War on Religion* (London: Darton, Longman & Todd, 2007) 71–73.

faith – put that destructive weaponry to good use, as they see it? On the basis even of this quite minimalist approach to morality, then, it ought to be perfectly clear that those scientists who furnished Hitler with the twentieth-century weaponry and communications technology that he put to such destructive use were culpable too for the evil consequences that occurred; and those atheistic scientists who continue to produce weapons of mass destruction – biological, chemical and nuclear – share in the guilt when fanatics of various kinds, religious and otherwise, order their use.²³

The Dynamics of Condemnation

Dawkins's treatment of the stance of religion towards other moral issues is no less simplistic, following the same pattern manifest above of pinning as much of the blame as possible for evil onto religious groups, while absolving others entirely. Homosexuality is an interesting case in point. From a Darwinian perspective, he explains, 'our brains are set up to enjoy sex because sex, in the natural state, makes babies' (169 [197]). Hence, 'an intelligent couple can read their Darwin and know that the ultimate reason for their sexual urges is procreation' (221 [253]). Nobody should be in any doubt, then, that sexual behaviour 'is about making babies, even on those occasions where contraception or homosexuality seems to belie it' (166 [194]). From the strict Darwinian perspective adopted by Dawkins here in relation to sexuality, therefore, it is patently clear that homosexual practice, as going against the entire movement of natural selection, constitutes at best a misreading of the evidence and at worst vainglorious folly in resisting the evolutionary process. In treating the issue, however, he finds yet again another angle for condemning religious believers – in this case, for their intolerance of homosexual acts undertaken 'in *private*'

23   See McGrath, *Dawkins' God,* 114–116.

(289 [327]) and for the ill-treatment and persecution of homosexuals that often arise as a result.

The dynamics of condemnation manifest in Dawkins's own stance in relation to this issue are particularly revealing, for even in this instance when religious believers finally manage to get something right and align with Darwinian considerations, he still succeeds in finding grounds for denouncing them and for absolving those who get the evidence spectacularly wrong and who either ignore or choose to oppose natural selection. It is thus somewhat difficult to take seriously those passages where Dawkins, without a trace of irony, condemns religious moralisers (who for once get the scientific evidence right and support it) for the detrimental consequences of condemning the detrimental consequences of homosexual practices that – notwithstanding their subversion of natural selection as a 'cumulative one-way street to improvement' (141 [169]) – can have no detrimental consequences because they are undertaken in private.[24]

As indicated previously, Dawkins states that he is against religious faith because it subverts science and ignores the evidence. However, by finding grounds to condemn religious faith even when it gets the evidence right, he compromises the integrity of his own arguments. Furthermore, by treating even moderate religious belief, backed up by rational theological argumentation, as a seedbed for fanaticism of every kind and by completely ignoring the evidence that religion might at least have done some good or conferred some benefits (however small, they might be) he finally undermines his own case in quite a spectacular manner.

This becomes clear when he argues quite forcefully that without the malign influence of religion, the enmity and violence that divide rival groups from one another in troubled areas of the world most likely would not occur. Although he acknowledges that large numbers of derogatory

24   Another example along the same lines is his treatment of the biblical story of Lot's escape from Sodom and Gomorrah. Where Lot might plausibly be praised for reading correctly the evidence of an impending natural disaster, Dawkins chooses to focus instead on the perverse moral standards of Lot and his dysfunctional family (239–241 [271–273]), with the aim of ridiculing biblical morality for considering Lot to be a righteous individual.

terms derive from non-religious sources – 'Frog, Wop, Dago ...' (269 [305]), again it is precisely the ones that derive from religion that cause trouble in the world: for religion is highly divisive, 'a *label* of in-group/ out-group enmity and vendetta ... often available when other labels are not' (259 [294]). Hence, in troubled places like Northern Ireland, 'without religion there would be no labels by which to decide whom to oppress and whom to avenge' (259 [294]).[25] Where then, it has to be asked, does that leave his own approach that has furnished us with no shortage of labels with which to characterise religious believers and their beliefs: for example, absolutist, dangerous, delusional, extremist, fundamentalist, fanatical, perverse, smug, terrorist-facilitating and violent-prone? Perhaps recognising that he is close to becoming 'hoist by his own petard', Dawkins would have us believe that the labels he applies to religion are entirely oriented towards peace and that 'such hostility as I or other atheists occasionally voice towards religion is limited to words' (281 [318]). And, of course, derogatory words directed by atheists against religion are entirely inconsequential; they never give rise to evil consequences, not even when uttered by such atheistic luminaries as Stalin or Chairman Mao! Dawkins is quite correct in highlighting 'the dark side of absolutism' (286 [323]), but the relativism he puts in its place has its own dark side and may have equally disastrous consequences.

In light of the above, the interpretative stance adopted by Dawkins emerges as a critical issue across several fronts. With regard to his presentation of passages from Scripture, for example, it has to be made clear that, methodologically speaking, his extremely literal way of reading those texts is quite fundamentalist. Though Dawkins himself is quite insistent that his own words have to be carefully interpreted – for example, 'selfish' is not to be understood as a moral quality – he has no qualms when it comes to reading the Bible about understanding words literally and ignoring the literary forms wherein they are found (for example, the difference

---

25   Eagleton remarks that Dawkins's comments on Northern Ireland simply betray
      'just how little he knows about it'. Eagleton, 'Lunging, Flailing, Mispunching', 4.
      See also Kathleen Jones, *Challenging Richard Dawkins: Why Richard Dawkins Is
      Wrong about God* (Norwich: Canterbury Press, 2007) 136.

between metaphor and fact, between poetry and historical narrative). His method of reading the Scriptures, in other words, is identical with the fundamentalist religious one he derides, the critical difference being that this latter approach to texts is grounded in a strict belief in an interventionist God while Dawkins's own approach to texts is predicated on the complete absence of belief in any God whatsoever.[26] Dawkins thus legitimates the fundamentalist approach to interpreting texts, but would he care for that method to be applied to his own text?

The question is by no means a facile one, given that more than enough passages can be found in *The God Delusion* to justify any amount of antagonism directed against the 'virus' of religious belief by those atheistically committed to eliminating it.[27] Indeed, contemporary studies of the phenomena of mass killing and genocide indicate how the perpetrators of such atrocities employ linguistic means to dehumanise their victims prior to acting. 'In the Holocaust', James Waller reminds us, 'the Nazis redefined Jews as "bacilli," "parasites," "vermin," ... and "plague.""[28] Against this background, it ought to be perfectly clear that labels of all sorts, including scientific ones, can be harnessed for destructive ends. It ought to be no less clear that Dawkins's interpretative stance towards the totalitarian regimes of the twentieth century is rather selective, to say the least.

---

26   Nicholas Lash describes the approach of Dawkins as fundamentalism 'in reverse'. See Lash, 'Where Does *The God Delusion* Come from?', 508; and Lash, *Theology for Pilgrims*, 3. See also McGrath, *The Dawkins Delusion*, 23.

27   See McGrath, *The Dawkins Delusion*, 50; also Cornwell, *Darwin's Angel*, 137–145.

28   James Waller, *Becoming Evil: How Ordinary People Commit Genocide and Mass Killing* (Oxford and New York: Oxford University Press, 2002) 246.

Naturally Selective

The problem of interpreting evidence in a highly selective manner crops up again and again in the course of *The God Delusion*. It can be found, for example, in the argument put forward by Dawkins that not even the 'smallest evidence'(273 [309]) exists that atheism systematically influences people to carry out evil actions and that, even though Stalin was an atheist, 'there is no evidence that his atheism motivated his brutality' (273 [309]). However, as anyone with even the skimpiest knowledge of history knows and as Alister McGrath pointedly makes clear, far from being consistent with the historical facts, this approach is clearly that of 'an ivory-tower atheist, disconnected from the real and brutal world of the twentieth century'.[29]

McGrath goes on to point out that the oppressive Stalinist regime, in attempting to enforce its atheistic ideology had no qualms about systematically laying waste to churches and annihilating religious adherents of every persuasion between 1918 and 1941. 'The statistics make for dreadful reading. This violence and repression was undertaken in pursuit of an atheist agenda – the elimination of religion'.[30] Though Stalin himself apparently had a devout upbringing and was a seminary student for a period, he later did his utmost to suppress religious belief. Historians Lewis Siegelbaum and Andrei Sokolov fill in some of the details from the era:

> Supposedly at the initiative of the masses, a 'Godless Five-Year Plan' was proclaimed. Closing of churches became widespread, priests were arrested and exiled. By the mid-1930s the number of Orthodox sanctuaries was reduced to one-quarter of that of pre-revolutionary times. Quite often at church closings there were fights between Komosol members and believers, and cemeteries and grave markers were destroyed. Churches were converted into storehouses and clubs. In one a shooting gallery was opened, the icons serving as targets. A defining moment of the fight

29 McGrath, *The Dawkins Delusion*, 48.
30 McGrath, *The Dawkins Delusion*, 48; for other examples of bias on the part of Dawkins, see 59–63.

against religion was the blowing up of the Church of Christ the Savior in Moscow
in December 1931. It was one way of liquidating symbols of the 'hated old times'
and starting the 'socialist reconstruction of the capital.' Monasteries were closed,
their elaborate compounds reverting to prisons, reformatories for minors, and
exclusive Soviet institutions.[31]

In systematically attempting to eliminate religion from society, the
Stalinist regime spared no effort and availed of every means to discredit
Christian ideals and practices, now deemed to be completely obsolete
and irrelevant, having been superseded by the socialist utopia that was
coming into existence and taking shape around the 'personality cult' of
Stalin himself.[32]
    Needless to observe, the reality evoked by these passages is not
reflected in *The God Delusion*, where Dawkins conveniently skips over
the historical evidence that is at odds with the theory he propounds.
Not only does he bypass the explicitly atheistic stance of Marxism, along
with its Leninist and Stalinist offshoots, he fails too to advert to the
claims of many of its adherents to be engaged in a scientific enterprise
in the strict sense, solidly grounded on the most up-to-date science, not
least that of Darwin. Fellow scientist Paul Davies, however, concedes
what actually took place, as he recounts how atheists were among the
first to greet Darwin's theory with enthusiasm: 'Friedrich Engels, for
example, had this to say in a letter to Karl Marx in 1859: "Darwin, by
the way, whom I'm reading just now, is absolutely splendid. There was
one aspect of teleology that had yet to be demolished, and that has now
been done".'[33] Indeed, writes Hannah Arendt, 'Engels could not think of

31   Lewis Siegelbaum and Andrei Sokolov, *Stalinism as a Way of Life: A Narrative in
     Documents*, abridged edition, trans. Steven Shabad and Thomas Hoisington (New
     Haven and London: Yale University Press, 2004) 63.
32   See Michael Burleigh, *Sacred Causes: Religion and Politics from the European
     Dictators to Al Qaeda* (London: HarperPress, 2006) 326–327.
33   Davies, *The Goldilocks Enigma*, 265. See also Mary Midgley, *The Myths We Live By*
     (London and New York: Routledge, 2004) 78–79.

a greater compliment to Marx's scholarly achievements than to call him the "Darwin of history"'.[34]

It should also be noted at this point that Dawkins, in his presentation of the religious beliefs of Hitler's regime in Nazi Germany, is silent on the same regime's recourse to Social Darwinism, the political philosophy advocated by Herbert Spencer, who applied Darwin's theory of evolution to human societies and who coined the phrase 'survival of the fittest' in so doing. As Frederic J. Baumgartner explains, 'Hitler adopted Social Darwinism and pushed it to its extremes. A race becomes great by purifying itself of alien elements and warring against weaker races. War is good, because it is the means by which the fittest struggle and survive. The more war the races engage in, the stronger they become, until one race, the German, will emerge as the superrace...'[35] The events of the Second World War proved this interpretation of the theory of evolution to be entirely wrong, but not without enormous cost in human bloodshed and life.[36]

The question of the correct interpretation of data is no less acute in relation to other issues that go to the heart of the arguments put forward in *The God Delusion*, not least in relation to teleology. Dawkins views children as natural-born teleologists, a tendency which disposes them to assign purpose and intention to all sorts of natural phenomena, including 'to the weather, to waves and currents, to falling rocks' (184 [213]). By these standards, ironically enough, his whole approach is no less credulous; for, having eliminated purpose from natural realities, he promptly reintroduces it at the genetic level in another guise, that of selfishness, by giving centre stage to the 'selfish gene' as 'the unit of natural selection (i.e.

---

34   Arendt, *The Origins of Totalitarianism*, 597.
35   Frederic J. Baumgartner, *Longing for the End: A History of Millennialism in Western Civilization* (New York: St. Martin's Press, 1999) 210. See also the remarks of Arendt, *The Origins of Totalitarianism*, 235–236.
36   See the remarks of Terry Eagleton on Dawkins's 'Herbert Spencerish way' in 'Lunging, Flailing, Mispunching', 5. See also some comments on the earlier works of Dawkins by Mary Midgley, *Science and Poetry*, second edition (London and New York: Routledge, 2006 [2001]) 272–275.

the unit of self-interest)' (215 [246]). Though obviously not conscious in any human sense, the 'selfish' gene is clearly 'purposeful' enough to seek to ensure its own survival by making exact replicas of itself at the expense of its rivals in the genetic hierarchy.[37] So the question arises: from whence 'selfishness' finally? What actually renders the 'selfish' selfish? Does the 'selfishness' exhibited by genes have a basis at an even more fundamental level of materiality, on a par with other esoteric events routinely taking place at the quantum level of existence? Or is it simply that what Dawkins interprets as 'selfishness' is a misreading of an inherent directedness in all reality, which, to be understood correctly, has to be situated in a much broader and more open framework than the one he supplies?

In relation to the theory of memes furnished by Dawkins too, the underlying issue of how data is to be interpreted is critical. Taking genetic replication as a basic reference point, he presents memes as 'units of cultural inheritance' (191 [222]) that replicate in somewhat analogous fashion to genes, so that 'the memes that prevail will be the ones that are good at getting themselves copied' (196 [228]). Just as genes cooperate and different kinds of gene cartels emerge, so memes, which are not necessarily good survivors on their own, cooperate to form 'memeplexes' that help to ensure their survival (see 197–201 [229–234]). As he develops this line of argument, it becomes increasingly clear that what he is actually trying to do is set in place a framework capable of furnishing biological answers to cultural and anthropological questions, all the while ignoring the fact that cultural anthropology and other similar disciplines are perfectly capable of supplying their own answers without recourse to the notion of memes. Not only is God reduced to the level of a scientific hypothesis, but it seems that every other aspect of life too can properly be brought within the ambit of scientific thought, now evidently the final arbiter of meaning and truth. Far from being insightful, this constitutes an exercise in reductionism that only succeeds in confusing the discussion, to the extent that the danger of reducing to meaningless nonsense all that

37   See James P. Mackey, *Christianity and Creation: The Essence of the Christian Faith and Its Future among Religions* (New York and London: Continuum, 2006) 384.

pertains to humanity is never far away.[38] Here again McGrath's critique is most enlightening and telling, as it highlights the tenuous nature of the evidence for the existence of memes and explains that

> The meme is a biological answer to an anthropological problem, and simply disregards and discounts the major successes of the discipline of anthropology in the explanation of cultural development – which took place without needing to bother with the unsubstantiated idea of a 'meme'. The meme is conceptually redundant... In *The God Delusion*, Dawkins sets out the idea of memes as if it were established scientific orthodoxy, making no mention of the inconvenient fact that the mainstream scientific community views it as a decidedly flaky idea, best relegated to the margins.[39]

John Gray is, if anything, even more withering in dismissing the notion of memes as scientific: 'Dawkins's "memetic theory of religion" is a classic example of the nonsense that is spawned when Darwinian thinking is applied outside its proper sphere... Talk of memes is just the latest in a succession of ill-judged Darwinian metaphors.'[40]

Given these highly significant criticisms of Dawkins's work, the question arises as to what exactly is going on when other scientists parrot the notion of memes, as if this pseudo-scientific, 'flaky idea' were established scientific fact. In his work, *The Goldilocks Enigma*, for example, the renowned physicist Paul Davies categorically states that 'memes play the same role in human culture that genes play in genetics. They may be, for example, habits, fashions or belief systems. Memes replicate, spread

38 See the critique of the whole notion of memes by Midgley, *Science and Poetry*, 95–107.
39 McGrath, *The Dawkins Delusion*, 43. As for the idea that religion is a 'virus of the mind', McGrath explains that this is 'not an idea that is taken seriously within the scientific community, and can safely be disregarded'. McGrath, *The Dawkins Delusion*, 41. See also the remarks of Jones, *Challenging Richard Dawkins*, 14–17.
40 John Gray, 'The Atheist Delusion', *The Guardian: Review* (Saturday, 15th March, 2008) 4–6, at 5. It is worth noting here too the comment of Freeman Dyson that 'now, after three billion years, the Darwinian interlude is over... Cultural evolution is not Darwinian'. Freeman Dyson, 'Our Biotech Future', *The New York Review of Books* LIV/12 (July 19, 2007) 4–8, at 4–6.

within the community and compete'.[41] Pushed to its logical conclusion, this stance means that the fashion for memes within certain parts of the scientific community is itself a meme. Hence, issues around circular argumentation and regress come to the fore once again, giving rise to questions such as the following: what meme underpins the fashion for memes? Or, as McGrath puts it, 'do we have to propose a meme for believing in memes in the first place?'[42]

McGrath's framing of the question is a critical one, for the phrase 'believing in memes' expressly links the issues of belief and memes. Is this linkage legitimate and if so, are we faced with the hitherto unthinkable: that perhaps Dawkins's anti-religious stance itself masks a form of belief? To the pursuit of that line of inquiry we must now direct attention in the next chapter.

41   Davies, *The Goldilocks Enigma*, 327, n.70.
42   McGrath, *The Dawkins Delusion*, 44.

CHAPTER 2

Believing in Disbelief

When people cease to believe in God, they don't believe in nothing; they believe in anything.
— G. K. CHESTERTON[1]

Ancient Stoic materialism is probably too much a piece of fantasy, too obviously unscientific, for the reason of modernity. In addition, its ethic was too sternly rational. You may, however, if you still belong to the earlier nineteenth century, choose mechanistic materialist monism. And you may update it a bit by the embellishment of a later evolutionism. In any case, your choice is atheism.
— JOHN COURTNEY MURRAY[2]

And yet we must not try to overstep the limitations by denying God, because that would also be the denial of humankind – with all its grave consequences. In fact, the question at stake here is: 'Do human beings really exist?'
— JOSEPH RATZINGER[3]

In the course of developing his arguments in *The God Delusion*, Dawkins makes the point that 'prejudices are indeed revealing giveaways of the date of a piece of writing' (269 [305]). Anyone seeking confirmation of that statement need look no further than the book itself, in which the

---

1   G. K. Chesterton, as quoted by Ronald B. Schwartz (ed.), *The Best Things Ever Said about God* (New York: Quill, 2000) 112.
2   John Courtney Murray, *The Problem of God: Yesterday and Today* (New Haven and London: Yale University Press, 1964) 93–94.
3   Ratzinger, *In the Beginning*, 86.

vehement one-sidedness of the arguments is a revealing giveaway that
something more than straightforward evidence drives the critique of religion. 'Conviction' and 'prejudice' might suitably be employed to express
what that 'something more' involves. In the final analysis, however, the
most appropriate words to characterise the hostile stance of Dawkins
towards religion are none other than 'belief' and 'faith' themselves.

The Beliefs of Dawkins

At first glance, the assertion that Dawkins's approach to religion is underpinned by belief appears to be quite ridiculous. After all, hasn't he explicitly
made clear his antipathy towards religious faith of every kind, considering
it to be a delusion of the worst kind with extremely evil consequences?
Furthermore, doesn't his very question – 'why would anyone go to war
for the sake of an *absence* of belief?' (278 [316]) – imply that the 'absence
of belief' is a defining characteristic of the atheistic worldview that he
and other scientists with their heightened consciousness espouse? Given
the dangers he sees inherent in faith stances of any kind, we might have
expected him to excise rigidly the language of belief in connection with
his own atheistic stance towards life and to replace it with more neutral
words, such as conviction or confidence or commitment. Surprisingly,
however, that is not the case, as a careful reading of *The God Delusion*
brings to the fore.

Scattered throughout his work are numerous instances where Dawkins
employs the language of belief to express his opinions. Included among
them are numerous 'creedal statements'[4] such as the following:

4   McGrath, *The Dawkins Delusion*, 48; see also 44.

'I *believe* the existence of God as a scientific hypothesis is, at least in principle, investigable' (105 [132]; emphasis added).

'... memes can sometimes display very high *fidelity* ...' (196 [227–228]; emphasis added).

'Perhaps I, too, am a Pollyanna to *believe* that people would remain good when unobserved and unpoliced by God' (228 [261]; emphasis added).

'I do not *believe* there is an atheist in the world who would bulldoze Mecca ...' (249 [283]; emphasis added).

From this point of view, Dawkins's criticisms of Fred Hoyle, the brilliant physicist and cosmologist, are particularly illuminating, because he indicates quite clearly that Hoyle's failure to appreciate natural selection lay not at the intellectual level but at the deeper level of belief: 'At an intellectual level, I suppose he understood natural selection. But perhaps you need to be steeped in natural selection, immersed in it, swim about in it, before you can truly appreciate its power' (117 [142–143]). So to appreciate natural selection fully, it seems, it is necessary even for great scientists to move beyond the intellectual level and acquire the type of 'immersion' that bears all the hallmarks of faith! Even for great scientists, in other words, a faith 'immersion' is a prerequisite to arrive at a correct understanding of scientific theories.

At one level, of course, there is nothing really surprising in this. A basic faith or confidence in reason's capacity to investigate the natural world is an intellectual requirement if that work is to be undertaken at all. As Mary Midgley observes, 'this kind of belief in a law-abiding universe – which is a real belief, not just a policy – is a precondition of any possible physical science'.[5] Scientific theories, then, cannot be defended

---

5   Mary Midgley, *Evolution as a Religion: Strange Hopes and Stranger Fears*, second edition (London and New York: Routledge, 2002) 127. The underlying issue here has long since been captured by the words of St Augustine: 'Faith, you see, is a step toward understanding; understanding is the well-deserved recompense of faith. The prophet says this plainly enough to all those who impatiently put the cart before the horse by looking for understanding and ignoring the need for faith. He says,

simply by treating them 'as if they were matters of direct experience. They
depend also on faith, on a choice about how to regard the universe. It must
follow, again, that faith is not just something to be got rid of, but something to be rightly directed.'[6] All this implies that even the scientific quest
for truth, much and all as it strives for objectivity, cannot stand outside
the critical hermeneutical circle, where the investigation of the material
world is inextricably linked with personal dispositions in an interpretative
context that involves mutual illumination and correction.[7]

Dawkins, of course, appears to anticipate this line of argument and
is entirely dismissive of it, considering it to be a 'tiresome red herring'
that a scientist's belief in evidence can be equated with fundamentalist
religious faith. Having to his own satisfaction dealt adequately with this
accusation elsewhere, he confines his response to a few brief remarks,
conceding in so doing that 'all of us believe in evidence in our own lives,
whatever we may profess with our amateur philosophical hats on' (282
[319]). Developing the argument briefly, he makes clear that the key to his
stance centres on the issue of evidence: 'We believe in evolution because
the evidence supports it … But my belief in evolution is not fundamentalism, and it is not faith, because I know what it would take to change
my mind, and I would gladly do so if the necessary evidence were forthcoming' (283 [320]). This denial, however, does not bring closure to the
issue, because, in defining his stance over against religion so rigidly, that
stance itself manifests a quasi-religious, highly ideological outlook that in
certain respects resembles what it denigrates, be it merely the Einsteinian
version of religion adopted by many scientists rather than the supernatural
version that he has rejected out of hand. The text of *The God Delusion*
helps to illustrate this.

Unless you believe, you shall not understand (Is 7:9, LXX)' St Augustine, 'Sermon
126', in *Sermons. The Works of Saint Augustine: A Translation for the 21st Century*,
Vol. III/4, trans. Edmund Hill, ed. John E. Rotelle (Brooklyn, New York: New
City Press, 1992) 270.

6   Midgley, *Evolution as a Religion*, 125.
7   See John Polkinghorne, *Quantum Physics and Theology: An Unexpected Kinship*
    (London: SPCK, 2007) 8–9.

Similar Symptoms

His own books, Dawkins makes clear, aspire to 'touch the nerve-endings of transcendent wonder that religion monopolized in past centuries' (12 [33]). Not only that, but the symptoms of 'love' experienced by those 'infected' by the religious 'virus' he condemns do not seem to be too different from the same symptoms experienced by those fully committed to the furthering of scientific knowledge. Compare the following statements:

'I made the comparison between falling in love and religion in 1993, when I noted that the symptoms of an individual infected by religion "may be startlingly reminiscent of those more ordinarily associated with sexual love. This is an extremely potent force in the brain, and it is not surprising that some viruses have evolved to exploit it" ...' (186 [216]).	'Maybe this is an aspect of what Carl Sagan meant when he explained his motive in writing *The Demon-Haunted World: Science as a Candle in the Dark*: "*Not* explaining science seems to me perverse. When you're in love, you want to tell the world. This book is a personal statement, reflecting my life-long love affair with science"' (366 [410–411]).

In sharp contrast to his love affair with science, Dawkins dismisses theology as a subject worthy of any serious study, considering its flavour to be 'characteristically obscurantist' (34 [55]) and having yet 'to see any good reason to suppose that theology ... is a subject at all' (57 [80]). So 'weird' and ludicrous are its teachings that ridicule is the only appropriate response to them, as the column on the left below indicates. In sharp contrast, however, contemporary science, in the form of quantum theory, is perfectly lucid in its 'queerness', thus calling forth praise as the corresponding column on the right makes clear!

'Thomas Jefferson, as so often, got it right when he said, "Ridicule is the only weapon which can be used against unintelligible propositions. Ideas must be distinct before reason can act upon them; and no man ever had a distinct idea of the trinity. It is the mere Abracadabra of the mountebanks calling themselves the priests of Jesus"' (34 [55]).

'Yet the *assumptions* that quantum theory needs to make, in order to deliver those predictions, are so mysterious that even the great Feynman himself was moved to remark ... "If you think you understand quantum theory ... you don't understand quantum theory." Quantum theory is so queer that physicists resort to one or another paradoxical "interpretation" of it' (365 [409]).

'The American philosopher Norman Malcolm put it like this: "The doctrine that existence is a perfection is remarkably queer ..."' (83 [107]).

'... the great biologist J. B. S. Haldane wrote, "Now, my own suspicion is that the universe is not only queerer than we suppose, but queerer than we can suppose ... I suspect that there are more things in heaven and earth than are dreamed of, or can be dreamed of, in any philosophy"' (364 [408]).

'To be fair, much of the Bible is not systematically evil but just plain weird...' (237 [268]).

'The biologist Lewis Wolpert believes that the queerness of modern physics is just the tip of the iceberg. Science in general, as opposed to technology, does violence to common sense' (366 [410]).

Other statements made by Dawkins invite comparison too, particularly in relation to the manner in which he takes every opportunity to cast aspersions on religious belief while celebrating the progress of science. For instance, he finds a source of great mirth and hilarity in Christian attempts to prove the existence of God, while contemporary scientific theories provoke a much more positive response – comedy and laughter!

'Even I, with my long experience, have never encountered wishful thinking as silly as that. I have, however, met many of the wonderful "proofs" … a richly comic numbered list of "Over Three Hundred Proofs of God's Existence". Here's a hilarious half-dozen …' (85 [109]).	'The dedicatee of this book made a living from the strangeness of science, pushing it to the point of comedy…. Laughter is arguably the best response to some of the stranger paradoxes of modern physics. The alternative, I sometimes think, is to cry.' (364 [408]).

The above examples, in fact, are but 'the tip of the iceberg', mere pointers to a far deeper issue lying beneath the surface: namely, the existence of the universe itself. Dawkins summarily dismisses the theist answer to the question of how the universe came to exist: he finds it 'deeply unsatisfying, because it leaves the existence of God unexplained' (143 [171]). Yet Dawkins himself has no qualms about leaving the existence of the universe unexplained, dismissing the ultimate question of why anything exists at all as illegitimate: 'What on earth *is* a why question? Not every English sentence beginning with the word "why" is a legitimate question' (56 [80]).[8]

So *The God Delusion* finally leaves us in the realm of mystery, with an unexplained fact which, if science cannot answer, cannot be answered

8   See the remarks of Lash, 'Where Does *The God Delusion* Come from?' 519–520; and Lash, *Theology for Pilgrims*, 16.

at all. We are thus at the threshold of the unexplainable, the nub around
which the book turns and the stumbling block on which it ultimately
falls. For here, at the very heart of his atheistic project, we finally come
face to face with the issue of faith: Dawkins's own personal faith which
underpins his stance towards religion and which, as has already been suggested above, influences the way in which he handles the very evidence
he prizes. In the vision he claims to espouse, everything hinges on the
evidence. Why then, as we have seen, does he seem to be quite choosy at
times about the type of evidence he is willing to consider legitimate?⁹ The
answer suggested by a close reading of the book, it seems to me, centres
on his monistic vision of life.

'Dyed-in-the-Wool' Monism

Mary Midgley makes the point that 'for scientists, as for anybody else,
incredulity is bound to be selective.'¹⁰ Dawkins acknowledges that most
atheists 'disguise their atheism behind a pious façade. They do not believe
in anything supernatural themselves, but retain a vague soft spot for irrational belief. They believe in belief' (353 [395]). It would not be an unrea-
sonable conclusion from these comments that Dawkins himself did not
believe in anything and that his stance was wholly objective, absolutely
reasonable and entirely devoid of belief.

It comes somewhat as a surprise, therefore, to read Dawkins confess-
ing that he is 'a dyed-in-the-wool monist' (180 [209]), one who actually
believes that the universe and all it includes, including human life itself,
has a purely natural, material basis. Julian Baggini's explanation, furnished
by Dawkins to explain this position, serves to make his beliefs very clear:
'What most atheists do believe is that although there is only one kind of

9   See McGrath, *The Dawkins Delusion*, 35.
10 Mary Midgley, *Science as Salvation: A Modern Myth and Its Meaning* (London
    and New York: Routledge, 1992) 90.

stuff in the universe and it is physical, out of this stuff come minds, beauty, emotions, moral values – in short the full gamut of phenomena that gives richness to human life' (13–14 [34]). Unlike those who acknowledge a fundamental distinction between matter and the human mind, Dawkins insists, 'a monist, by contrast, *believes* that mind is a manifestation of matter ... and cannot exist apart from matter' (179–180 [209]; emphasis added). He spells it out clearly:

> Human thoughts and emotions *emerge* from exceedingly complex interconnec-
> tions of physical entities within the brain. An atheist in this sense of philosophical
> naturalist is somebody who believes there is nothing beyond the natural, physical
> world, no *super*natural creative intelligence lurking behind the observable universe,
> no soul that outlasts the body and no miracles – except in the sense of natural
> phenomena that we don't yet understand. If there is something that appears to lie
> beyond the natural world as it is now imperfectly understood, we hope eventually
> to understand it and embrace it within the natural (14 [34–35]).

Dawkins's faith, then, is a purely natural phenomenon that is oriented to matter as the 'one kind of stuff in the universe' to which everything, including reason itself, is traceable and by which it is explainable. It is perfectly clear from this that a realm of pure spirit is by definition excluded from this worldview; spirit does not and cannot exist independently of matter; it is simply a particular dimension or realm of the material that has come to expression in human beings. This rejection of the independence of the spiritual realm from the material, it is now clear, is the underlying reason for his refusal to accept an ultimate spiritual basis for materiality; and it is this rejection too that underpins the questions he thinks finally trump spiritual belief: 'Who made God?' (109 [136] and 'who designed the designer'? (See 158 [188]).[11]

Dawkins's belief in evolution is not fundamentalism, he maintains, and it is not faith because he knows what it would take to change his mind and he 'would gladly do so if the necessary evidence were forthcoming' (283 [320]). While such a declaration of openness is highly commendable, it leaves us trapped once more in a vicious circle that requires nothing

---

11   On the latter question, see also Davies, *The Goldilocks Enigma*, 231–232.

short of a miracle in the strict sense of the term to break through and surmount.[12] For the monistic belief underpinning his scientific stance requires that the evidence Dawkins needs to change his mind has to be of the material kind; data of a purely 'spiritual' kind is worthless, totally incapable of meeting the strict standards of scientific evidence, because reality in its entirety – including the evidence in question – is ultimately reducible to the material. We can thus conclude that if he is to change his mind about evolution or, indeed, about religion, Dawkins requires that appropriate material evidence be furnished in support of the existence of a non-material realm. Furthermore, since he knows 'what it would take to change [his] mind' (283 [320]), we can conclude too that he knows exactly the type of natural, material evidence he needs to come to a belief that life involves more than the purely natural and material. We can only conclude that what Dawkins actually requires is something he has ruled out *a priori* – a miracle (see 14 [35]).

Darwinian natural selection provides the key to Dawkins's scientific faith in the natural as all-embracing and, within the worldview that he outlines, it fulfils a role that can only be described as 'god-like'. For gaps, which 'by default in the mind of the creationist, are filled by God' (128 [154]), by default in his mind are filled by natural selection, or by its equivalent in the physical realm: 'There is a butcher and a baker, but perhaps a gap in the market for a candlestick maker. The invisible hand of natural selection fills the gap' (197 [229]). And though science might struggle to explain some of the gaps that have arisen because 'the evolutionary intermediaries happen to be extinct' (301 [340]), we can be confident that as our knowledge grows so will the gaps correspondingly diminish, even though it would be 'utterly illogical to demand complete documentation of every step of any narrative, whether in evolution or any other science' (127 [153]).

12   From a theological point of view, it is important to stress that a miracle cannot simply be reduced to a violation of the laws of nature, as some would argue. For discussions of the issues, see Crean, *A Catholic Replies*, 50–61; and Terence L. Nichols, *The Sacred Cosmos: Christian Faith and the Challenge of Naturalism* (Grand Rapids, Michigan: Brazos Books, 2003) 183–198.

Raised Consciousness or Simply 'Old Hat' in New Guise?

For Dawkins, religion is an obstacle to enlightenment, a consciousness suppressor that retards human progress to such an extent that there are but few 'enlightened places' (357 [400]) to be found on earth. In sharp contrast, Darwin's theory of evolution by natural selection constitutes a powerful consciousness-raiser; it is, indeed, 'the ultimate scientific consciousness-raiser' (117 [142]), the means whereby true enlightenment is attained. Hence, scientists more than most have benefited from its power, for 'even now full understanding is confined to a minority of scientific specialists' such as biologists, who have had their consciousness raised by natural selection (220 [252]; see also 143–144 [172–173]). Dawkins quite modestly admits that his own consciousness 'has been raised by Darwin' (footnote, 145 [173]). On that basis, he makes quite clear in *The God Delusion* that his purpose 'is consciousness-raising' (3 [25]) and that he wishes to share the benefits of his insights with his readers, by raising their consciousness to the fact that all answers to the riddle of life formulated prior to 1859 are simply wrong (see 367 [411]).[13]

On the basis of these assertions, readers might reasonably surmise that the monism to which Dawkins adheres constitutes an entirely new and revolutionary stance towards life; a philosophy hitherto unimagined and unimaginable because the key to it, natural selection, was not discovered until Darwin came on the scene. Far from that being the case, however, monism might actually be described as 'old hat'; for this vision of life and of the world is as old as philosophy itself, articulated first in ancient Greece in the earliest days of philosophy several centuries before Jesus Christ. Granted that monists in those days knew nothing of natural selection and its power for consciousness-raising, it is staggeringly amazing

---

13   For a further elaboration of this topic, see Richard Dawkins, *The Selfish Gene*, second edition (Oxford and New York: Oxford University Press, 1989 [1976]) 1 and 267. See also Linda Wiener and Ramsey Eric Ramsey, *Leaving Us to Wonder: An Essay on the Questions Science Can't Ask* (Albany: State University of New York Press, 2005) 41–43.

that, several thousand years ago, those who adhered to this philosophy succeeded in reaching conclusions that emphasised the primacy of matter and explained all reality in purely materialist, almost 'Dawkinsian', terms. In a comment that might have been written with *The God Delusion* in mind, but is actually directed towards the Sophist philosophy which was expounded in the fifth century before Christ, Richard Tarnas writes: 'In the end, they argued, all understanding is subjective opinion. Genuine objectivity is impossible. All a person can legitimately claim to know is probabilities, not absolute truth… Hence the Sophists concluded in favour of a flexible atheism or agnosticism in metaphysics and a situational morality in ethics'.[14] In the atomistic worldview espoused by Democritus and Leucippus around the same time, the world was composed exclusively of uncaused and unchanging material atoms, the infinite number of which ceaselessly moved in a boundless void, colliding and combining to provide the phenomena of the visible world. 'What was real was matter in space, atoms moving randomly in the void. When a man died, his soul perished; matter, however, was conserved and did not perish… By implication of these early philosophical forays, not only the gods but the immediate evidence of one's own senses might be an illusion, and the human mind alone must be relied upon to discover rationally what is real'.[15] The general thrust of the Hellenistic mind in those early years, then, was to shift the focus from the spiritual realm to the natural, so that 'a naturalistic science matured in step with an increasingly skeptical rationalism'.[16]

In light of the above, it ought to be fairly clear that contemporary science shares many presuppositions in common with Greek philosophy in its distant origin. This point is again well made by Tarnas, who explains that the atomistic worldview re-emerged in Renaissance Europe, there to impact decisively on scientific thinking that was slowly beginning to call

---

14   Richard Tarnas, *The Passion of the Western Mind: Understanding the Ideas that Have Shaped Our World View* (London: Pimlico, 1991) 27–28, 29.
15   Tarnas, *The Passion of the Western Mind*, 22. See also Mary Midgley, *The Myths We Live By*, 29.
16   Tarnas, *The Passion of the Western Mind*, 23. See also See Midgley, *Science and Poetry*, 80–94.

religious thought on cosmological and other related matters into question. Many of the tenets of the mechanistic and materialistic worldview of the ancient Greeks, he suggests, enjoyed 'an unexpected validation in the theoretical conclusions and philosophical tenor of the Scientific Revolution and its aftermath. A similar restoration would come to the Sophists, whose secular humanism and relativistic skepticism found renewed favor in the philosophical climate of the Enlightenment and subsequent modern thought'.[17] Against this philosophical background, the upshot of Dawkins's argument is nothing less than that Darwinian natural selection has vindicated a view of life that was prevalent long before Christianity came on the scene. So much for raised consciousness and so much for his criticism of theology that it has 'not moved on in eighteen centuries' (34 [55]); in light of the foregoing analysis, it seems that the raising of human consciousness envisaged by Dawkins entails buying into a worldview that is firmly stuck even further back in the past.

Critical questions arise at this point: if the description of reality furnished by monism is so obviously correct and if the Greeks actually had it correct in the earliest days of philosophy, then why on earth did they themselves feel the need to move beyond it in the first place? How did they so lose the run of themselves that human learning subsequently went horribly wrong and that another couple of thousand years would pass before human thought could be set on the right track again by the scientific Enlightenment and Darwinian naturalism? The obvious answer to these questions, in keeping with the anti-religious thesis Dawkins has propounded, is that the religious 'virus' somehow came to insinuate itself strategically in the Greek psyche at a vulnerable moment to derail it from the right path and to bring enormous misery over time to the human community, until other genes at work in the mind of Darwin pointed him in the right direction and he successfully managed to get things back on the right track in 1859. From a more historical standpoint, however, a very different answer can be given: that the Greeks felt the need to move on because the materialistic, mechanistic view of life that

---

17   Tarnas, *The Passion of the Western Mind*, 293–294; see also 265–271.

had been propounded by the early philosophers not only failed to do justice to the whole of life but actually had quite serious detrimental consequences for the community as a whole. Richard Tarnas is again quite illuminating on this point:

> The Sophists' relativistic humanism, for all its progressive and liberal character, was not proving wholly benign. The larger world opened by Athens's earlier triumphs had destabilized its ancient certainties and now seemed to require a larger order – universal, yet conceptual – within which events could be comprehended. The Sophists' teachings provided no such order, but rather a method for success. How success itself was to be defined remained moot. Their bold assertion of human intellectual sovereignty – that through its own power man's thought could provide him with sufficient wisdom to live his life well, that the human mind could independently produce the strength of equilibrium – now seemed to require reevaluation. To more conservative sensibilities, the foundations of the traditional Hellenic belief system and its previously timeless values were being dangerously eroded, while reason and verbal skill were coming to have a less than impeccable reputation. Indeed, the whole development of reason now seemed to have undercut its own basis, with the human mind denying itself the capacity for genuine knowledge of the world.[18]

Thus it was in the early days of Greek philosophy and, most surprisingly given Dawkins's stated position on the nature of reality, thus it seems to be once more in our own time, as the concluding chapter of *The God Delusion* strikingly bears witness.

Reality: More Science Fiction than Fact?

In the final chapter of his work, Dawkins directs his attention to the human need for wonder and consolation, seeking to break the stranglehold that religion has traditionally exercised over these aspects of the

---

18   Tarnas, *The Passion of the Western Mind*, 30–31.

human psyche by affirming the life-enhancing role of science and evoking the sense of exhilarating freedom that scientific knowledge brings. In so doing, however, he says enough to suggest that the strictly monistic vision of life he has hitherto advocated is seriously lacking in several respects.

The problem to which I am alluding emerges in connection with an image employed by Dawkins to describe our puny insignificance in a world of immense scope, where the human view of the whole is restricted to the extremely narrow window of visible light and where the human imagination is desperately ill-equipped to deal with the vastness of the world. The image in question is 'the mother of all burkas' (362 [405]), which can also be described in cavern-like terms: 'We live near the centre of a cavernous museum of magnitudes, viewing the world with sense organs and nervous systems that are equipped to perceive and understand only a small middle range of sizes, moving at a middle range of speeds...' (363 [407]).[19] Against the background of Greek philosophy as discussed above, that particular image is quite illuminating, for it echoes the very ancient one of the cave, utilised by Plato in comparing this world to the shadows falling on its wall. Richard Tarnas explains.

> In the *Republic*, Plato illustrated the difference between authentic knowledge of reality and the illusion of appearances with a striking image: Human beings are like prisoners chained to the wall of a dark subterranean cave, where they can never turn around to see the light of a fire that is higher up and at a distance behind them. When objects outside the cave pass in front of the light, the prisoners mistake as real what are merely shadows created on the wall. Only one who is freed from his chains and leaves the cave to enter into the world beyond can glimpse true reality, though when first exposed to the light he may be so overwhelmed by its dazzling luminosity as to be unable to recognize its actual character... For Plato, then, the great task facing the philosopher was to emerge from the cave of ephemeral shadows and bring his darkened mind back into the archetypal light, the true source of being.[20]

19   See the criticisms of this image, from a feminist theological perspective, in Beattie, *The New Atheists*, 65–69.
20   Tarnas, *The Passion of the Western Mind*, 41–42. See also Davies, *The Goldilocks Enigma*, 4.

It ought to be clear from this that far from evoking or defending a version of materialistic monism, as Dawkins employs his image of the burka to do, Platonic philosophy actually resists and undermines it. For in the Platonic scheme of things, the material cosmos as we know it is fleeting, ephemeral and far from perfect. Beyond the confusion, the imperfection, temporality and unreality of this world, however, exists the absolute, timeless and perfect order on which it is shaped: the real world of transcendent, ideal Forms that are entirely objective and exist as transcendent entities in their own right. Thus, knowledge gained by the senses is seriously flawed, while true knowledge is gained only when we move beyond the senses to a direct, intellectual apprehension of the ideal Forms through philosophical reflection, of which mathematics is a key component.[21]

The Platonic worldview provides an important backdrop against which to read the closing presentation of Dawkins in *The God Delusion*, in which the issue of 'reality' itself emerges as a critical question to be addressed. After a brief consideration of quantum theory and some of the quite bizarre interpretations of it put forward by leading scientists, he makes the point that 'our brains have evolved to help our bodies find their way around the world on the scale at which those bodies operate' (368 [412]). Thus, as 'evolved denizens of Middle World' (369 [414]) – to be contrasted with the 'Micro World' at which bacteria, for example, operate – 'it is useful for our brains to *construct* notions like solidity and impenetrability, because such notions help us to navigate our bodies through a world in which objects – which we call solid – cannot occupy the same space as each other' (368 [413]). Against the background of his previously stated adherence to monism, Dawkins leaves us with a conundrum concerning the relationship between mind and matter: for, on the one hand, while matter is but 'a useful construct' (370 [415]) of mind in Middle World, on the other hand, mind itself is but 'a manifestation of matter' (179 [209]).

---

21   See Tarnas, *The Passion of the Western Mind*, 6–12. See also Joseph Ratzinger, *Eschatology: Death and Eternal Life*, trans. Michael Waldstein (Washington, D.C.: The Catholic University of America Press, 1988) 77–78.

The view of reality that Dawkins propounds with this circular argumentation enables one to re-read with fresh insight those passages of *The God Delusion* where he marvels 'at the richness of human gullibility' (36 [57]) fostered by religion, while decrying its bizarre superstitions and rituals that foster a disengagement from the real world. Again a side-by-side comparison of some of his 'scientific' criticisms of religion, on the basis of its 'unreality', with some of his lauding of science, even though it does 'violence to common sense' (366 [410]), is most illuminating.

'That is really all that needs to be said about personal "experiences" of gods or other religious phenomena. If you've had such an experience, you may well find yourself believing firmly that it was real. But don't expect the rest of us to take your word for it ...' (92 [117]).	'"Really" isn't a word we should use with simple confidence.... "Really", for an animal, is whatever its brain needs it to be, in order to assist its survival. And because different species live in such different worlds, there will be a troubling variety of "reallys"' (371 [416]).
'My own feeling, to the contrary, would have been an automatic, deep suspicion of any line of reasoning that reached such a significant conclusion without feeding in a single piece of data from the real world' (82 [107]).	'What we see of the real world is not the unvarnished real world but a *model* of the real world, regulated and adjusted by sense data – a model that is constructed so that it is useful for dealing with the real world' (371 [416–417]).
'It is possible to conceive, Anselm said, of a being than which nothing greater can be conceived. Even an atheist can conceive of such a superlative being, though he would deny its existence in the real world' (80 [104]).	'We have this tendency to think that only solid, material "things" are "really" things at all' (370 [415]).

Having had our consciousness raised by Dawkins that the word "'really" isn't a word we should use with simple confidence', that there are actually 'a troubling variety of "reallys"' and that what 'we see of the real world is not the unvarnished real world but a *model* of the real world', it becomes clearer still that his confident dismissal of God on the basis of the *real* evidence he supplied in the earlier part of the book is far from what he claims it to be. Monistic his underlying vision might ostensibly be, but with the above affirmations he leaves us in some doubt about matter as real and materialistic naturalism as a coherent description of what is real.

At this point, it is worth considering how a Platonic view of reality has many adherents among those at the cutting edge of contemporary science and mathematics. Many mathematicians, Paul Davies writes, 'believe that mathematical objects have real existence, yet are not situated in the physical universe. Theoretical physicists, who are steeped in the Platonic tradition, also find it natural to locate the mathematical laws of physics in a Platonic realm'.[22] One such mathematician, Roger Penrose, writes on the issue as follows:

> Whether we look at the universe at the quantum scale or across the vast distances over which the effects of general relativity become clear, then, the common-sense reality of chairs, tables and other material things would seem to dissolve away, to be replaced by a deeper reality inhabiting the world of mathematics... Might mathematical entities inhabit their own world, the abstract Platonic world of mathematical forms? It is an idea that many mathematicians are comfortable with... To a mathematical Platonist, it is not so absurd to seek an ultimate home for physical reality within Plato's world. This is not acceptable to everyone... My own position is to avoid this immediate paradox by allowing the Platonic mathematical world its own timeless and locationless existence, while allowing it to be accessible to us through mental activity. My viewpoint allows for three different kinds of reality: the physical, the mental and the Platonic-mathematical, with something (as yet) profoundly mysterious in the relations between the three.[23]

22   Davies, *The Goldilocks Enigma*, 14.
23   Roger Penrose, 'What is Reality?' *New Scientist*, 50th Anniversary Special 1956–2006, 192/2578 (18 November 2006) 32–39, at 38–39. In this special edition of the magazine, the opening article by Michael Brooks and bearing the title, 'In Place of God', carries details of a conference in California at which Dawkins was among

Against this background, which for all its sophistication still succeeds in avoiding the profoundly mysterious, spiritual dimension of reality, Dawkins's materialistic naturalism comes across as rather simplistic, to say the least, with serious repercussions for the credibility of his entire argument.

The Semi-Illusion on the Delusion

The issues raised in the preceding paragraphs are far from academic or trivial, for at stake is not merely the denial of God but the denial of several other realities too, with huge ramifications for human existence itself and for our way of living in the world. The hard-edged Darwinian stance adopted by Dawkins brings these issues very clearly to the surface.

In the course of his critique of religion in *The God Delusion*, one of the key issues dealt with and summarily dismissed by Dawkins is the religious stance towards the human self. 'Many religions', he points out, 'teach the objectively implausible but subjectively appealing doctrine that our personalities survive our bodily death. The idea of immortality itself survives and spreads because it caters to wishful thinking. And wishful thinking counts, because human psychology has a near-universal tendency to let belief be coloured by desire ...' (190 [220–221]). In sharp contrast to such illusory thinking, he goes on to argue, science makes clear to us that there is a fundamental continuity between all forms of life, both animal and plant, and with material reality itself. Hence,

> The granting of uniquely special right to cells of the species *Homo sapiens* is hard to reconcile with the fact of evolution... A better way to say this is that there are no natural borderlines in evolution. The illusion of a borderline is created by the fact

the leading participants arguing for the need for secular science to oust religious belief. On the Platonic world and science today, see Davies, *The Goldilocks Enigma*, 14–17, 266–274.

that the evolutionary intermediaries happen to be extinct. Of course, it could be argued that humans are more capable of, for example, suffering than other species. This could well be true, and we might legitimately give humans special status by virtue of it. But evolutionary continuity shows that there is no *absolute* distinction. Absolutist moral discrimination is devastatingly undermined by the fact of evolution (300–301 [339–340]).[24]

Human life itself, then, is of no intrinsic worth and the human self ultimately comes to nothing, as is evident from his reflections on the issue of 'assisted suicide'. Arguing that being dead is really no different from being unborn, Dawkins states quite categorically: 'When I am dying, I should like my life to be taken out under a general anaesthetic, exactly as if it were a diseased appendix. But I shall not be allowed that privilege, because I have the ill-luck to be born a member of *Homo sapiens* rather than, for example, *Canis familiaris* or *Felis catus*' (357 [400]). So, in his scheme of things, human life straddles a very narrow line between 'luck', on the one side, and 'ill-luck', on the other. Having had recourse to 'major infusions of luck' (141 [169]) to account both for the success of evolution in leading to human existence in the first place and then in allowing it to develop, it now transpires that when sickness and suffering strike, when old age arrives and when death beckons, the 'luck' that was our lot as members of the human species literally flips over to become its opposite, the aptly described 'ill-luck', thereby leaving our condition more wretched and pitiable than ever. Just how wretched and pitiable it actually is can be gauged from Dawkins's use of computer imagery to describe the human mind.

Our brains, Dawkins suggests, are 'on-board computers' (367 [412]; see also 179–180 [209]) and they run 'first-class simulation software' (88 [113]). Even though initially it 'was constructed and debugged by natural selection' (361 [405]), however, this software can still go awry, misfire and

---

24   As to why the evolutionary intermediates should be extinct, it seems that many species as they evolved consumed less complex species, thereby eliminating most, if not all, traces of their own evolution. See Robert Hazen, 'What Is Life?' *New Scientist*, 50th Anniversary Special 1956–2006, 192/2578 (18 November 2006) 46–51, at 49.

give rise to some extraordinary illusions, the most pernicious of them all being called 'God'. Unfortunately, it is patently clear from the arguments Dawkins presents that the debugging process has been spectacularly unsuccessful, for most people on planet earth, being religious, have succumbed to the religious 'virus', rendering them easy prey for delusory thinking that only the most enlightened of atheistic scientists, who *believe* wholeheartedly in natural selection, have successfully avoided or overcome. But what if even that scenario is too optimistic and that, apart altogether from any nonsensical talk about God, life as even scientists experience and describe it is finally illusory too, merely a 'virtual' simulation of reality rather than reality itself? What if scientific reason's faith in scientific evidence is ultimately unfounded and all our scientific certainties are nonsensical illusions anyway? Though Dawkins does not pursue this line of inquiry, he does note that 'science-fiction authors ... have even suggested (and I cannot think how to disprove it) that we live in a computer simulation, set up by some vastly superior civilization' (73 [98]). Even that suggestion, it now appears, has entered the scientific mainstream, to judge by an article of Nick Bostrom (that appeared alongside the aforementioned one by Roger Penrose) in which he treats seriously the proposition that we are almost certainly living in a computer simulation. Though he acknowledges it may not be correct, for other possibilities have to be considered too, if indeed it is correct, he states,

> you are almost certainly living in a computer simulation that was created by some advanced civilisation. What Copernicus and Darwin and latter-day scientists have been discovering are the laws and workings of the simulated reality. These laws might or might not be identical to those operating at the more fundamental level of reality where the computer that is running our simulation exists (which, of course, may itself be a simulation). In a way, our place in the world would be even humbler than we thought.[25]

25   Nick Bostrom, 'Do We Live in a Computer Simulation?' *New Scientist*, 50th Anniversary Special 1956–2006, 192/2578 (18 November 2006) 38–39, at 39. For yet other angles to this, see Davies, *The Goldilocks Enigma*, 203–216; Ward, *Why There Almost Certainly Is a God*, 14–15; and Paul Broks, 'What is Consciousness?'

By comparison with this scenario, Dawkins's problems with the wishful
and illusory thinking fostered by religion and outlined in the course of
The God Delusion seem mild indeed. For, in the event of this scenario
being correct, not only would we not exist in the way we think we do, but
neither would the world; and the only things Dawkins holds faithfully
secure in spite of everything, immortal genes and the scientific reason that
guarantees there are at least some enlightened people about to guide the
rest of us in our ignorance, would themselves be revealed as completely
misfiring, distorted and ungrounded.

Straddling the divide between 'luck' and 'ill-luck' is the least worrying
of the balancing acts bequeathed to us by Dawkins, then, for the dividing
lines between enlightenment and irrationality, between the 'real' and the
'virtual' and between 'firmly grounded' and 'wholly simulated' seem even
more insecure and dangerous on which to perch. Yet still more precarious
is the human self's own identity in a world where quantum relationships
have a determining impact at every level of reality.[26] One of the interpretations of quantum theory to which Dawkins gives credence is the
multiverse one, which 'postulates a vast and rapidly growing number of
universes, existing in parallel and mutually undetectable except through
the narrow porthole of quantum-mechanical experiments. In some of
these universes I am already dead. In a small minority of them, you have
a green moustache. And so on' (365 [409]).[27] So, in this awe-inspiring

---

New Scientist, 50th Anniversary Special 1956–2006, 192/2578 (18 November 2006)
56–61.

26 Scientists now claim to understand how the classical world emerges from the
quantum world. See Martin Chown, 'Forever Quantum', *New Scientist* 193/2595
(17 March, 2007) 36–39.

27 Dawkins is by no means the only scientist who adopts this position. Paul Davies,
for example, outlines the implications of the theory for us as follows: 'But by the
remorseless logic of statistics, for every Earth containing an identical you there
will be countless more Earths with a being differing from you only in some slight
respect, such as hair colour or height, or last year's birthday present. The cosmologist Max Tegmark of the Massachusetts Institute of Technology has worked out
that the average distance to the nearest identical you should be about 10 to the
power 10^{29} metres, ... But even if you need not fear an encounter with a duplicate

scenario of parallel worlds in a multiverse of fluid simultaneity and infinite self-possibility, the human 'I' completely fragments, dissolves and evaporates, as it is forced to straddle any amount of worlds, only a tiny minority of them 'friendly places' (374 [419]).

In the last analysis, Dawkins's 'I' or 'me', the rational self or denizen of Middle World, is no more real or solid than the brain in which it is contained and the material ground on which we ostensibly stand. Just as matter is merely a construct, so the self is purely virtual, wrought by the complex interactions of microscopic particles and the chemical reactions to which they give rise. Thus, the 'innate dualism' that is deeply ingrained in all of us – giving rise to 'the idea that there is a *me* perched somewhere behind my eyes' (180 [210]²⁸) and predisposing us 'to believe in a "soul" which inhabits the body rather than being integrally part of the body' (181 [210]) – is simply wrong; for no 'I' or 'me' can exist independently of materiality. Though he does not develop the argument any further in *The God Delusion*, in an earlier work Dawkins explicitly pointed to the illusory nature of human subjectivity when comparing it to the individual organism, which though 'not exactly an illusion ... is a secondary, derived phenomenon, cobbled together as a consequence of the actions of fundamentally separate, even warring, agents'.²⁹ On this basis, he floats the idea that 'perhaps the subjective "I", the person that I feel myself to be, is the same kind of semi-illusion ... a cobbled, emergent, semi-illusion analogous to the individual body emerging in evolution from the uneasy cooperation of genes'.³⁰

---

you, the very notion that there could be not just one, but an *infinity* of identical copies of you, leading identical lives (and infinitely many others leading similar but not identical lives) is deeply unsettling...' Davies, *The Goldilocks Enigma*, 202. See also Keith Ward, *The Big Questions in Science and Religion* (West Conshohocken, Pennsylvania: Templeton Foundation Press, 2008) 231–235; and Ward, *Why There Almost Certainly Is a God*, 67–82.

28   The word 'me' is italicised in the first edition of the book, but not in the second.

29   Richard Dawkins, *Unweaving the Rainbow: Science, Delusion and the Appetite for Wonder* (London and New York: Penguin Books, 1998) 308.

30   Dawkins, *Unweaving the Rainbow*, 308–309. See also Midgley, *Science and Poetry*, 4.

A 'semi-illusion' or a 'full-blown' one or, best of all, just another 'delusion' that even puts 'God' in the shade – it can hardly *matter* at the end of the day, for the self has no intrinsic worth and is of no ultimate concern, because the 'semi-illusion' of Dawkins can be dead in this world and in several more, while still shaving its green moustache in some other one and perhaps combing its golden locks in yet another, and so on *ad infinitum.* Thus does the 'dyed-in-the-wool monist' finally outdo religion, trumping in every respect the simplistic religious tendencies of all 'natural born dualists and teleologists' who – unaware of the vast multitude of their identical and variant selves existing in parallel in other regions of the multiverse – are prone to fancifully believing in the existence of a soul or disembodied spirit, which 'can easily be imagined to move on somewhere else after the death of the body' (181 [210]; see also 180 [209]). Ultimately, then, the self as postulated by Dawkins is as unreal as God; this 'semi-illusion' is arguably the basic and, in some respects, the most insidious and pernicious form of the God delusion.

Defending a Unique Self in a Real World

With the self evaporated, all talk about 'reason' and 'evidence' and 'objectivity' becomes not merely suspect but completely irrelevant, for, in the last analysis, life as we know and experience it is but an illusion of some sort or other.[31] Even the best case scenario *The God Delusion* leaves us with, on ostensibly scientific grounds, bears all the hallmarks of a séance: a 'semi-illusion' (Dawkins's own self) communicating with other 'semi-illusions' (the selves of the rest of us) in order to issue a warning about a 'delusion' (God). If that is what scientific objectivity finally amounts to, then we are truly the most pitiable of all creatures, trapped in a type of

31   Interestingly enough, in this context, the caption on the front cover of *New Scientist* 193/2595 (17 March, 2007) reads: 'Reality Is an Illusion: Why We Are Blind to the Quantum Truth'.

superstition that is utterly nonsensical for considering itself reasonable and that can only lead to madness in some form or other.

It would be worthwhile at this point to reflect on the following words of Thomas Berry, with respect to scientific endeavours over the past two hundred years:

> During this period the human mind lived in the narrowest bonds it has ever experienced. The vast mythic, visionary, symbolic world with its all-pervasive numinous qualities was lost. Because of this loss, we made our terrifying assault upon the earth with an irrationality that is stunning in enormity, while we were being assured that this was the way to a better, more humane, more reasonable world.[32]

Berry's argument is quite straightforward: that scientific thought, for all the progress and insights gained, has been so narrowly focused and so arrogantly developed that what passes for rationality often simply masks its opposite. *The God Delusion* offers little in the way of hope that this catastrophic approach will be rectified soon.

In addition to the dissolution of reason that accompanies the dissolution of the self, all talk of human freedom simply becomes nonsensical too. For freedom as thus envisaged is nothing other than a coming to terms with the tension involved in the high-wire act, wherein the human individual, controlled by the genes at war within the body and the brain, is left to dangle precariously, between 'luck' and 'ill-luck', between materiality and virtuality, and between the rationality of a tiny handful of enlightened specialists and the irrationality of the multitude in a world that is monistic, deterministic and purposeless, and where various forces predetermine every outcome: mathematical probability at the quantum level; natural selection as 'the invisible hand' (197 [229]) filling every gap in Middle World; and, at the cosmic level, the vagaries of 'multiversal' by-laws (see 145 [173–174]) as yet undiscovered but that just happen to be 'anthropic' in this particular universe which we 'commonsensically'

---

32   Thomas Berry, *The Dream of the Earth* (San Francisco: Sierra Club Books, 1988) 134–135. See also Tony Kelly, *An Expanding Theology: Faith in a World of Connections* (Newtown, NSW: E. J. Dwyer, 1993) 31.

suppose is real and where nonsensically (or, perhaps, comically) we think we are.

Yet, strangely enough and no doubt irritatingly enough for its proponent, even this bleak scenario offers some consolation to the religious believer. For given the infinite number of other universes sanctioned by the multiverse hypothesis, then, as Keith Ward observes, 'there will be universes in which pink elephants endlessly dance gavottes and other universes in which unicorns and mermaids really do exist... Everything will be true somewhere'.[33] Hence, in terms of the images furnished by Dawkins, not only does a universe in which I have a green moustache exist, but there is another in which I have a head of red hair, and so on and on. Hence, too, there almost certainly exists one where I am flying about joyfully in the type of 'celestial teapot' derided as nonsensical (within the parameters of this world only) in the course of *The God Delusion* (51–54 [74–77]). And, undoubtedly, in another one I am held in the arms of a God of incomparable love who lavishes divine gifts in abundance on me, risks all on me, even to the extent of becoming human like me with a view to saving me and ultimately deifying me in a realm of heavenly bliss that lasts forever. This, indeed, is exactly the scenario which is taught by Christian faith. It is taught, however, not with reference to another world, but to the one in which we actually live: this world, brought into existence through the mysterious act of the Creator God, who out of the infinite variety of worlds that could possibly exist actually brought this one into existence; this vast universe which contains a tiny planet in which life has evolved in miraculous fashion over billions of years, underpinned by divine power and evolving under divine guidance by means of a whole host of physical processes, including natural selection and many others as yet undiscovered. Adapting the terms of Schrödinger's parable of the cat (365 [409–410]), though they are far from adequate for the task, the mind of God grasps every possible world; but it is this one that God looks on with love and actually 'opens', thereby triggering the collapse of the

---

33   Ward, *The Big Questions in Science and Religion*, 233.

probability 'wave function' and effecting a singular event: the divine act of creation that is ongoing, still unfolding in our presence.[34]

This, then, is the world in which human selves are not only unique and real, but they have been endowed with a capacity to reach out and respond to the God who never ceases to come to them in myriads of ways, inviting them to a relationship of intimate love that is to last forever. This, to put it simply, is the world which God created and in which God subsequently became human in Jesus Christ to transform and redeem it and to divinise it in the glory of the resurrection.

34   See Neil Ormerod, 'Chance and Necessity, Providence and God', *The Irish Theological Quarterly* 70/3 (2005) 263–278, at 277–278. See also Bernard J. F. Lonergan, *Insight: A Study of Human Understanding*, third edition (New York: Philosophical Library, 1970) 662–663.

CHAPTER 3

From Absurdity to Meaning

The purpose of this book is to show that complete objectivity as usually attributed to the exact sciences is a delusion and is in fact a false ideal.
— MICHAEL POLANYI[1]

A little philosophy inclineth a man's mind to atheism, but depth in philosophy bringeth men's minds about to religion.
— FRANCIS BACON[2]

As a matter of fact, the doctrine that Might is Right needed several centuries (from the seventeenth to the nineteenth) to conquer natural science and produce the 'law' of the survival of the fittest.
— HANNAH ARENDT[3]

Though *The God Delusion* poses many critical questions for faith, its own inherent contradictions seriously undermine its credibility as an adequate, let alone comprehensive and coherent, approach to life. Though purporting to be wholly objective in outlook and strictly scientific in its approach, it is manifestly prejudiced in its critique of religious belief, going for overkill more than for an objective evaluation of positive evidence, even when such evidence is demonstrably available. The pseudo-scientific rhetoric that accompanies the scientific argument ultimately proves its

---

1   Polanyi, *Personal Knowledge*, 18.
2   Francis Bacon, as quoted by Dan Hind, *The Threat to Reason: How the Enlightenment Was Hijacked and How We Can Reclaim It* (London and New York: Verso, 2007) 61.
3   Arendt, *The Origins of Totalitarianism*, 212.

own undoing, as it becomes clear that the very theories Dawkins advances stand in contradiction with the materialistic monism that supposedly underpins them. In the final analysis, something has to give: either reality itself or the credibility of his approach; and, as the previous chapter sought to demonstrate, it is very much the latter that is found wanting as a coherent description of the former.

Yet though his approach is quite simplistic at times, the issues Dawkins raises are quite profound, for they concern nothing less than the understanding of the universe and of our place in it. In this respect, his stance reflects the dominant cosmology of our age: a scientific worldview that can be traced back several centuries to the 'Copernican Revolution', which displaced the earth from the centre of the universe, thereby overturning the ancient cosmology derived from Greek philosophy and the Hebrew Scriptures. Subsequent discoveries, both theoretical and practical, not only confirmed but reinforced the whole thrust of that worldview, which views the cosmos as wholly explainable in scientific terms and seeks to furnish the requisite explanations for every process that occurs.

Over the past few centuries, science has enjoyed immense success in its endeavours to explain the universe and all its processes. In so doing, it has succeeded in opening up vast new vistas in terms of our understanding of the world and of life in general. It has brought enormous benefits to the human family as a whole, helping to improve the quality of life for most people. The extraordinary discoveries it has made in practically every field of research have been immensely enriching and the technological achievements that have resulted have improved prospects for countless people.

Yet the progress has not been without a downside, for the scientific understanding that has been gained has not always been employed towards just and peaceful ends. Indeed, the more that understanding has grown, the more correspondingly has the power for domination, so that scientific knowledge and technology have proved to be as effective in helping the powerful to trample on the weak as in improving the quality of life for everybody. Dawkins is quite right in highlighting the violence to which religion can lead. But when science becomes ideological and degenerates into scientism – *'that science is the proper and exclusive foundation for thinking about and answering every question*[4] – then, the result is really no different, as the violence of the twentieth century, fuelled by the destructive weaponry made possible by scientific advances, aptly demonstrates.

I. Scientific 'Isms'

Scientific success in explaining this world has been predicated on approaching it in a strictly empirical fashion and seeking to understand nature purely on its own terms. This approach goes back to the dawn of modernity and to the inductive scientific method, advanced by Francis Bacon, which came to the fore from the sixteenth century onwards. In terms of his understanding, the scientific method hitherto practised was fundamentally flawed; it actually foreclosed progress, by relying on deductive reasoning that gave priority to an abstract, predetermined order, into which it attempted to force natural phenomena, however poorly the fit between them. The ancient and medieval assumption that the natural order was underpinned by the divine will and permeated with a divine purpose – readily accessible to the human mind and expressible in terms of four causes, material, efficient, formal and final – was in fact a hindrance to a genuine human understanding, the true key to which was attention to and observation of things as they actually were. Thus, Bacon argued, knowledge ought to be pursued inductively, with painstaking and unbi-

4   Wiener and Ramsey, *Leaving Us to Wonder*, 15; see also John C. Polkinghorne, *One World: The Interaction of Science and Theology* (Philadelphia and London: Templeton Foundation Press, 2007 [1986]) 73. On the scientism of Dawkins and other contemporary atheists, see John F. Haught, *God and the New Atheism: A Critical Response to Dawkins, Harris, and Hitchens* (Louisville, Kentucky, and London: Westminster John Knox Press, 2008) 11, 17–19, 30, 38 and 63–64.

ased attention to and analysis of concrete data, to reach general conclusions supported by empirical evidence and experimentation.[5]

The Scientific Revolution

Bacon's claims paved the way for a scientific revolution to which illustrious thinkers such as Galileo, Descartes and Newton made an immense contribution. So successfully did the theories they elaborated explain the natural world and its processes that they quickly established the basis for a new worldview, a mechanistic one that placed human reasoning centre stage while relegating God to the periphery.[6] Whereas previous generations of thinkers had looked on nature as a symbol of the divine, the more scientists now probed its regularities and articulated the laws underpinning them, the less they needed to resort to divine guidance and intervention for explanations. As a result of these developments, natural religion came to displace revealed religion and many thinkers came to conceive the relationship between God and the world in terms of either pantheism or deism: the former identifying God with the whole of reality, the latter a form of rational religion holding a conception of God as a benevolent architect, clockmaker or absentee landlord, who, having brought the world into existence, thereafter allowed it to operate according to its own natural rhythms and laws.[7] By harnessing those laws to their own advantage, human beings could then act on the world to improve

5   See Tarnas, *The Passion of the Western Mind*, 272–275; Midgley, *Science and Poetry*, 56–57; and Oliver Davies, *The Creativity of God: World, Eucharist, Reason* (Cambridge and New York: Cambridge University Press, 2004) 2, 52–58. For some critical remarks, see the encyclical letter on Christian hope by Pope Benedict XVI, *Spe Salvi* 16–25; Jones, *Challenging Richard Dawkins*, 56–57; and Beattie, *The New Atheists*, 60–65.
6   See Tarnas, *The Passion of the Western Mind*, 248–271.
7   See Walter Kasper, *The God of Jesus Christ*, trans. Matthew J. O'Connell (London: SCM Press, 1983) 22–24.

their lot, with the eventual result that 'progress' became a rallying cry and
commerce the engine for revolution in every sphere of life.

The latent tendency to atheism in both pantheism and deism gradually became explicit in the materialistic naturalism prevalent in the
natural sciences from the eighteenth century onwards. The evolutionary
worldview, initially propounded by Charles Darwin, marked a decisive
milestone in this respect, for, as *The God Delusion* amply demonstrates,
it allowed scientists to jettison the last remnants of the metaphysical and
religious baggage that had for so long hampered their investigations. No
longer hidebound by notions of formal and final causality attributable
to divine agency, they were now free to focus their energies on the concrete, empirical data furnished by the world, to probe the mechanisms
and elaborate the laws of nature in a professedly objective manner. That
claim to objectivity has thus come to define scientific method. Jacques
Monod puts it like this: 'The cornerstone of the scientific method is the
postulate that nature is objective. In other words, the *systematic* denial
that "true" knowledge can be reached by interpreting phenomena in
terms of final causes – that is to say, of "purpose."'[8] According to him,
'for science the only *a priori* is the postulate of objectivity,'[9] so that 'the
systematic confrontation of logic and experience is the sole source of
true knowledge'.[10]

Granted that scientific endeavours have proved to be remarkably
successful in furnishing explanations for natural phenomena of every
kind, the approach is not without its downsides, quite serious ones too.
Those downsides begin to become apparent in the characteristic double-
edged stance of scientific thought towards other disciplines. On the one
hand, science stands solitary and alone, claiming to safeguard rationality
while standing over against and distinguishing and separating itself from
every discipline that fails to match its claims to intellectual rigour and

8   Monod, *Chance and Necessity*, 30.
9   Monod, *Chance and Necessity*, 98.
10   Monod, *Chance and Necessity*, 154. See the critical remarks of this position in
     Joseph Ratzinger, *On the Way to Jesus Christ*, trans. Michael J. Miller (San Francisco:
     Ignatius Press, 2005) 63–65; and in Midgley, *Science and Poetry*, 47–48.

objectivity. And, on the other hand, science is presented as normative for those disciplines too, on the basis of its 'omni' competence with respect to every aspect of life, as if everything and everybody, every thought and every faculty, every dimension of meaning and every truth can finally be reduced to a scientific formula that scientists alone can comprehend and authentically interpret. Far from being wholly scientific, objective and value-free, as its claimants imply, that all-embracing claim is an imperialist one that is historically, socially and culturally conditioned.[11] It is also, to adapt the words of Mary Midgley, a highly bizarre metaphysical claim that seeks to 'out-Descartes Descartes', that seriously lacks coherence, that is laden with prejudice and that is derived from philosophical and theo-logical positions traceable back to ancient times.[12] It is, in brief, a highly ideological stance in the sense articulated by Hannah Arendt: 'Ideologies – isms which to the satisfaction of their adherents can explain everything and every occurrence by deducing it from a single premise.'[13] Though of relatively recent vintage, she goes on to explain, 'ideologies are known for their scientific character: they combine the scientific approach with results of philosophical relevance and pretend to be scientific philosophy.'[14]

Atomism and Reductionism

Atomism, the notion that the best way to understand any reality is to break it up into it smallest component parts, has long been a characteristic of human thought. As we have already seen in the previous chapter, this approach originated in Greek thought and it was intimately linked with materialism, the notion that matter alone is real. Though this reductionis-tic viewpoint ultimately failed to satisfy Greek philosophers, it has seen a

11   See Colin J. D. Greene, *Christology in Cultural Perspective: Marking out the Horizons* (Grand Rapids, Michigan: Eerdmans, 2003) 282–286, esp. 283.
12   See Midgley, *Evolution as a Religion*, 24; see also Midgley, *Science and Poetry*, ix–xii.
13   Arendt, *The Origins of Totalitarianism*, 603.
14   Arendt, *The Origins of Totalitarianism*, 603–604.

remarkable resurgence in modern times, to the extent that it is now quite a fashionable ideology and quite a formidable tool in the ongoing struggle of atheism against religious influence in every sphere of life.[15] Among the firm exponents of this approach is Daniel Dennett, who holds that 'Darwin's dangerous idea is reductionism incarnate, promising to unite and explain just about everything in one magnificent vision'.[16]

The extraordinary success of the reductionistic approach in the physical sciences has been the catalyst for similar endeavours in other fields, not least in relation to the investigation of human life itself. In these terms, as already indicated with respect to the views expounded by Dawkins in *The God Delusion*, the human mind itself is ultimately reducible to matter and its operations to the dynamic interactions of the particles that constitute it, according to laws as yet undiscovered. Thus, as Mary Midgley observes, neurology and evolutionary biology have become choice vehicles utilised in pursuit of 'a dream of taming and simplifying our inner life so that it will somehow conform to the known laws of matter and will stop setting us problems of its own'.[17] That pursuit and dream, she goes on to argue, are not without serious consequences, not least in the social atomism or individualism that claims scientific status for the political idea that 'only individuals are real while the groupings in which they live are not'.[18]

An intriguing variation of this approach is the 'cultural atomism' championed by Dawkins in his theory of memes, which he describes as 'units of cultural inheritance' (191 [222]) that replicate in analogous fashion to genes and that come to exercise a dominant role in the shaping of human thought. This position means that everything hitherto understood to be proper to other disciplines – including history, philosophy, psychology and law, not to mention religion and the study of it – can be traced

---

15   See Midgley, *Science and Poetry*, 80–94; also John F. Haught, *God after Darwin: A Theology of Evolution* (Boulder, Colorado, and Oxford: Westview Press, 2000) 60.

16   Daniel C. Dennett, *Darwin's Dangerous Idea: Evolution and the Meanings of Life* (London and New York: Penguin Books, 1995) 82.

17   Midgley, *Science and Poetry*, 3.

18   Midgley, *Science and Poetry*, 3; see also 95–96.

to these fundamental cultural units, the meaning of which and the final verdict on which pertains to science alone.[19] Hence, as Midgley observes, those other disciplines are finally but 'dubious entities on the borders of science proper, becoming respectable only when they manage to imitate real science closely. Thus the strange composite intellectual entity called science now turns out to be not just omnicompetent but unchallenged, the sole form of rational thinking'.[20]

Far from being a purely material substance that can be broken down into basic units of whatever sort, however, human culture in all its facets – including language, habits, ideas, beliefs, customs, laws, artefacts, symbols, values and even the scientific process itself – is charged with meaning; meaning that is wrought by the dynamic interrelatedness of human beings in freedom, which, inherited biological characteristics notwithstanding, cannot finally be equated with or reduced to the replication of identical material units or to the movement of particles.[21] Even from the standpoint of the biological sciences, the atomistic approach is fatally flawed, as becomes clear when one considers the example, furnished by Midgley, of a botanist who attempts to identify a leaf.

> This botanist does not simply mince up the leaf, put it in the centrifuge and list the resulting molecules. Still less, of course, does he list their constituent atoms, protons and electrons. Instead, he looks first at its structure and considers the possible wider background, asking what kind of tree it came from, in what ecosystem, growing on what soil, in what climate, and what has happened to the leaf since it

19   The Einsteinian approach to religion, which some scientists champion and which Dawkins at least tolerates (see 13–19 [33–41]), can be interpreted along these lines too. Corey S. Powell describes this approach as 'sci/religion', and he describes how it 'offers a positive and immensely appealing alternative way to look at the world, a religion of rational hope'. Powell, *God in the Equation*, 253. 'Sci/religion', according to Powell, is revelatory and it even has redemptive power: '... the Temple of Einstein does have something to say about how to go to heaven – not as a guide to the afterlife, but metaphorically as a guide to living a moral life'. Powell, *God in the Equation*, 254.

20   Midgley, *Science and Poetry*, 209; see also 162–169 and 183–185.

21   See Midgley, *Science and Poetry*, 100.

left its tree? This 'holistic' approach is not folklore but as central and necessary a part of science as the atomistic quest.[22]

What applies to the leaf applies likewise to every other ecosystem and living organism. The complex ecosystem that is a wood, for example, cannot simply be reduced to the list of trees, plants and wildlife found in it. Indeed, far from being a conglomeration of discrete entities that bear no relation to one another, the wood is constituted rather by a whole series of overlapping ecosystems dynamically interacting with one another, continually supporting and nourishing one another to the benefit of all. Such is the intricate nature of their interrelationships that to take them apart in piecemeal fashion is literally to 'miss the wood for the trees'.[23]

Against this background, three general remarks seem in order. First, given that neither the atom nor the gene are finally closed systems and that the laws governing their interactions in wholes greater than themselves can never be entirely deduced from their properties in isolation, a wholly reductionistic approach to reality is fundamentally flawed. What is required rather is a much more holistic approach that respects not only the integrity of the specific entity but also its openness to unite with other entities to form entirely new ones that are greater than the sum of their parts.[24] Second, rather than seeking an all-encompassing scientific explanation for culture in all its richness and diversity, it is far more enlightening to view that particular quest itself as but a particular cultural phenomenon, best understood by situating it in the context of contemporary Western rationality. Third, the self-defeating character of scientific reductionism becomes apparent when its focus is directed towards human beings themselves in the attempt to solve the elusive problem of consciousness.

---

22   Midgley, *The Myths We Live By*, 29. On the problems that arise from approaching the social sciences in a mechanistic fashion, see Midgley, *Science and Poetry*, 158–169.

23   See John F. Haught, *Christianity and Science: Toward a Theology of Nature* (Maryknoll, New York: Orbis Books, 2007) xiii.

24   See Pannenberg, *Toward a Theology of Nature*, 21–23, 37–41; also Nichols, *The Sacred Cosmos*, 142–151.

Objectivism

At the heart of Western rationality since modern times began is an emphasis on objectivity that is seen as the defining characteristic of scientific reason and method, as wholly dedicated to the study of objects and wholly guided by the objective evidence available to rational inquiry. Yet, though such an approach has proved immensely successful in practical terms, it is becoming increasingly clear that methods appropriate to the study of objects alone can take matters only so far. Even physics, the most abstract and objective of the sciences, has come to see that the subjective decisions and actions of an observer play a central role in the outcome of experiments at the quantum level. Not only does the human subject influence the world, then, but objectivity itself both presupposes and is open to subjectivity – the conscious self that is capable of adopting a particular stance towards the world – a fact which demands that the sciences treat people not merely as objects but as subjects too. Putting the matter rather bluntly, then, to attribute total objectivity to scientists in the pursuit of evidence even in the exact sciences is to make a claim that cannot be upheld.[25] By these standards, and to turn the argument of Dawkins completely on its head, the pure scientific objectivity by which he declares God to be a delusion is itself quite delusory.[26]

The questions that arise at this point are quite disconcerting, for the claim to scientific objectivity as it is practised leaves us no option but to accept that a mindless, purposeless universe has by an unimaginable fluke given rise to the mindful, purposeful subjectivity that makes that very objectivity possible. As Paul Davies puts it, 'somehow the universe

---

25   Arendt notes that scientists, no less than anybody else, are not immune from ideological thinking. She observes, for example, that 'today no single science is left into whose categorical system race-thinking has not deeply penetrated'. Arendt, *The Origins of Totalitarianism*, 212.

26   See the words Michael Polanyi, quoted at the beginning of this chapter, from *Personal Knowledge*, 18. See also Midgley, *The Myths We Live By*, 54–55; Haught, *God and the New Atheism*, 5–6, 82–84; Haught, *God after Darwin*, 166–169; and Ward, *Why There Almost Certainly Is a God*, 95–96.

has engineered, not just its own awareness, but its own *comprehension*. Mindless, blundering atoms have conspired to make, not just life, not just mind, but *understanding*.[27] Mind and understanding, in these terms, have no other basis in reality than wholly mindless materiality; they are ultimately grounded not in mind but in the mindlessness which is a defining characteristic of materiality in its primordial state. It is arguable, however, that, far from being objective, such an approach to reality amounts merely to objectivism of the crudest variety. That becomes quite clear when the issue of consciousness, which the objective stance towards life actually presupposes, is investigated.

To the thoroughgoing reductionist, John Polkinghorne points out, the answer to the perpetual puzzle of the connection of mind and brain 'is easy: mind is the epiphenomenon of brain, a mere symptom of its physical activity'.[28] This is another viewpoint for which Daniel Dennett argues: 'The prevailing wisdom, variously expressed and argued for, is *materialism*: there is only one sort of stuff, namely *matter* – the physical stuff of physics, chemistry, and physiology – and the mind is somehow nothing but a physical phenomenon. In short, the mind is the brain'.[29] To Polkinghorne, however, that point of view is a highly curious one to adopt, for 'the most basic experience we have is mental, that stream of consciousness which constitutes what is sometimes called our I-story'.[30] That 'stream of consciousness' is qualitatively different from all other phenomena, precisely because it is that which enables all of us, includ-

<hr>

27   Davies, *The Goldilocks Enigma*, 5.

28   Polkinghorne, *One World*, 109. Mary Midgley describes epiphenomenalism as 'the steam-whistle theory of mind'. See her discussion of the topic in Midgley, *Science and Poetry*, 146–157, at 149.

29   Daniel C. Dennett, *Consciousness Explained* (London and New York: Allen Lane. The Penguin Press, 1991) 33. For some relevant remarks on this approach, see Haught, *Christianity and Science*, 138–139; John Hick, *The New Frontier of Religion and Science: Religious Experience, Neuroscience and the Transcendent* (Houndmills, U.K., and New York: Palgrave Macmillan, 2006) 56; and Davies, *The Goldilocks Enigma*, 259–263.

30   Polkinghorne, *One World*, 109.

ing scientists themselves, to adopt an objective stance towards all other phenomena.

Mary Midgley explains that consciousness 'is not just one more phenomenon. It is the scene of all phenomena, the place where appearances appear. It is the viewpoint from which all objects are seen as objects. The first set of questions that arise about it are questions about ourselves.'[31] In confronting those questions, it has to be recognised that since an objective account of consciousness has to presuppose the very thing it seeks to account for, objectivity itself turns out 'to be a will o' the wisp. Thus there is not just one problem of consciousness nor could there be a single "science of consciousness" to deal with it'.[32] The implications of these observations for the scientific enterprise itself are clearly drawn out by Polkinghorne:

> The reductionist program in the end subverts itself. Ultimately, it is suicidal. Not only does it relegate our experiences of beauty, moral obligation, and religious encounter to the epiphenomenal scrapheap. It also destroys rationality. Thought is replaced by electro-chemical neural events. Two such events cannot confront each other in rational discourse. They are neither right nor wrong. They simply happen. If our mental life is nothing but the humming activity of an immensely complexly connected computerlike brain, who is to say whether the program running on the intricate machine is correct or not? ... If we are caught in the reductionist trap, we have no means of judging intellectual truth. The very assertions of the reductionist himself are nothing but blips in the neural network of his brain....[33]

These types of arguments, however, are but minor irritants to those who, knowing that science works and that it achieves concrete results which cannot be matched by other disciplines, pursue their highly ideological endeavours to encompass all human knowledge under the ambit of scientific reason. As *The God Delusion* amply demonstrates, the conviction

31   Midgley, *Science and Poetry*, 114.
32   Midgley, *Science and Poetry*, 165. See also Kelly, *An Expanding Theology*, 109–114; Ward, *Why There Almost Certainly Is a God*, 16–17; and Beatrice Bruteau, *God's Ecstasy: The Creation of a Self-Creating World* (New York: Crossroad, 1997) 156.
33   Polkinghorne, *One World*, 110.

that 'science alone suffices'[34] is alive and well in scientific circles and it continues to underpin much scientific research today.

Totalism

Scientific claims and endeavours to hegemony are perhaps nowhere more apparent today than in the pursuit of a so-called 'theory of everything'.[35] Understood purely in the limited sense of an attempt to unify the laws of physics insofar as physicists now understand them, work on such a theory has much going for it, in that it holds out the possibility of deepening our understanding of the universe and of our place in it. Understood, however, in a totalising manner as the complete, definitive and final explanation of the universe as a whole and of all life, such a theory is quite simply unacceptable.[36]

One way of approaching the issues at stake is to consider how the very expression, 'theory of everything', allows a gap to open between 'theory' (as pertaining to the non-material realm of ideas that furnishes explanations) and 'everything' (identifiable with materiality as a whole and requiring explanation). Materialistic naturalism of the type argued for by Dawkins and other scientists, however, finally rejects that gap, closing it firmly by holding 'everything' – including 'theory' and its language and concepts – to have a purely material basis and the mind to be completely reducible to the physical brain.[37] Among the problems associated with this position is one suggested by the very title of Daniel Dennett's book in which he expresses and defends the above views, *Consciousness Explained*;

34 Haught, *God after Darwin*, 19. See also Arendt, *The Origins of Totalitarianism*, 603–606.
35 See Midgley, *The Myths We Live By*, 61–67; McGrath, *The Dawkins Delusion*, 9; and Cornwell, *Darwin's Angel*, 63–67. See also Michio Kaku, 'Will We Ever Have a Theory of Everything?' *New Scientist*, 50th Anniversary Special 1956–2006, 192/2578 (18 November 2006) 62–65.
36 See Haught, *Christianity and Science*, 6–7.
37 See the discussion above on objectivism. See also Dawkins, 179–180 [208–210].

for this expression brings to the fore an absolutely basic question that can be posed to every scientific explanation *ad infinitum* – what explains the explanation? It is quite clear that the universe is scientifically comprehensible, but that fact itself requires explanation. Discerning readers will have noted that the above question is but a variation of the 'knockout' question Dawkins thinks he has delivered to religious belief – who designed the designer? (see 109 [136] and 158 [188]).[38] Having identified the problem of infinite regress as the critical factor undermining religious faith, no one ought to be in denial that the contemporary scientific quest has to confront an identical hurdle.

A second approach to the issues at stake centres on the adequacy of the basic categories employed by scientists as they attempt to exercise dominance in every sphere of learning. Much as our knowledge of the world and of material processes has grown since the scientific revolution, it would be a grave mistake on our part to think that we are the first to have to deal with questions such as the ones discussed above. Though much of what contemporary science brings to the discussion is new, the critical underlying issues can be traced back to discussion in early Greek philosophy, which came to recognise that matter never stands alone but in its very constitution is penetrated by 'form' to such an extent that it is always 'in-formed'. The implications of this are immense, for it means that the information pursued by science is not an irrelevant abstraction, but rather inheres concretely in nature, underpinning and helping to 'form' every actuality. John Haught explains:

> Form or pattern, as philosophers from Aristotle to Whitehead have noted repeatedly, is a metaphysical aspect of things, one without which they would have no actuality at all. Informational patterning, in other words, is a *metaphysical* necessity; for in order for anything to be actual at all, it must have at least some degree of form, order, or pattern. Otherwise a thing would be indefinite, and whatever is indefinite is no-thing. To be *some-thing* at all an entity has to be informed in a definite way... But if information were literally taken out of the world, then the world and its inhabitants – at all levels – would cease to be at all. Neither would

38   See McGrath, *The Dawkins Delusion*, 9–12.

there be atomic units, for these too must be patterned, limited, and 'informed' to be actual themselves.[39]

The importance of these insights comes to the fore with regard to the work of Dawkins in connection with the materialistic monism that he espouses, insisting there is 'only one kind of stuff in the universe and it is physical' (13–14 [34]). How this 'one kind of stuff', evidently mindless and completely uni-form in every respect, managed to set in motion within itself a process leading to the evolution of a breathtaking array of information-laden units capable of being understood by minds that emerge out of the process, is a question not answered by him. His insistence too that the gene is the 'archetypal replicator' – a replicator being 'a piece of *coded information* that makes exact copies of itself' (191 [222]; emphasis added) – would seem to stand in direct contradiction to that view by prioritising information over simple materiality. After all, as Midgley reminds us, 'each particular gene dies in the cell it belongs to'.[40] No individual gene is immune from the death and decay that is the lot of every living organism to which it belongs; what is critical and what continues to endure, long after individual genes have decayed, is the 'information' that is transmitted from one generation to the next.

The problem of circularity previously identified as a characteristic of Dawkins's work comes to the fore with a vengeance at this point, for the 'theory of everything' so beloved of scientists will fall short of the universality demanded by 'everything', if it fails to be self-grounding, self-incorporating, self-explanatory and self-validating. Paul Davies touches on the issue in observing that 'the universe clearly cannot be self-explanatory without containing the ability to explain itself!'[41] Strictly speaking, then, the 'theory of everything' itself has to be included in the 'everything'

---

39   Haught, *God after Darwin*, 76. On the scientific approach to matter since the time of Descartes, see Midgley, *Science and Poetry*, 6–17 and 185–186.

40   Midgley, *Evolution as a Religion*, 145. Midgely is here responding to the claim made by Dawkins in an earlier work that the 'genes are the immortals'. Dawkins, *The Selfish Gene*, 34.

41   Davies, *The Goldilocks Enigma*, 289; see also 236; and Midgley, *The Myths We Live By*, 19–20.

theorised about, if the theory is not to be patently absurd and incomplete. Intriguingly, this opens up a rather 'Anselmian' way of approaching the whole issue, for it suggests that the 'everything' in the 'theory of everything' can be taken as but another way of saying 'that than which more cannot be thought'. Expressed in these terms, the so-called 'theory of everything' not only bears all the hallmarks of the 'logomachist trickery' (81 [105]) with which Dawkins characterises Anselm's reasoning in the ontological argument, but actually succeeds in putting it considerably in the shade; for, pushed to the limits in this manner, the 'theory of everything' finally amounts to a 'theory of that than which more cannot be thought' – in short, a 'theory of itself'. Strange as it may seem, that is nothing other than the question of God, 'the Unmeasurable who can be measured only by himself',[42] as the phrase of Hans Urs von Balthasar indicates.

Determinism and Utilitarianism

Much and all as scientists strive to be objective, even their quest for truth cannot stand outside the critical hermeneutical circle, where the investigation of the material world is inextricably linked with personal dispositions in an interpretative context that involves mutual illumination and correction.[43] Scientific thinking itself is neither value free nor presuppositionless, so that scientists in their pursuit of objective knowledge cannot finally evade grappling with deep philosophical issues that human thought has struggled with long prior to the emergence of Christianity. Indeed, their failure to do so and to take a critical stance towards the ideological positions underpinning their work simply involves the gigantic risk of repeating the past too, in all its glorious mistakes and folly. Far from being

42   Hans Urs von Balthasar, *The Glory of the Lord: A Theological Aesthetics*, Vol. I. *Seeing the Form*, trans. Erasmo Leiva-Merikakis, ed. John Riches (Edinburgh: T & T Clark, 1982) 473.
43   See Polkinghorne, *Quantum Physics and Theology*, 8–9; also Midgley, *Evolution as a Religion*, 33–39 and 124–127.

value free and truly liberating, then, scientific thought is value laden in a manner that is often quite deterministic with respect to every sphere of life, including even the future; for a rigid determinism of this kind holds that complete information on the complete state of the world at any particular instant would allow an individual with the required competence to predict what happens next with scientific exactitude.[44]

Determinism today, Mary Midgley explains, comes in many forms, all of them vying with one another for supremacy as the key to understanding life: 'genetic determinism, economic determinism, neurological determinism and so forth – where the claim seems to be that a single discipline has finally found the engine which runs all the other causes'.[45] In the vision of things elaborated by Dawkins, for example, the key determinants in human life and activity can be found in the genes, the hidden agents which, selfishly 'programmed' to replicate themselves at every opportunity, constitute 'the invisible hand' (197 [229]) at every step in the lives of all of us, who are merely 'their survival machines'.[46] To express it in imaginative terms, human beings are nothing more than 'puppets dangling on strings', fully controlled and guided by their genes, in the guise of puppeteers. Dawkins himself adopts a mechanistic image to communicate the same point: 'By dictating the way survival machines and their nervous systems are built, genes exert ultimate power over behaviour. But the moment-to-moment decisions about what to do next are taken by the nervous system. Genes are the primary policy-makers; brains are the executives....'[47]

44 On this question, see Hick, *The New Frontier of Religion and Science*, 112; Lonergan, *Insight*, 132; Neil Ormerod, *Creation, Grace, and Redemption* (Maryknoll, New York: Orbis Books, 2007) 12; Ormerod, 'Chance and Necessity, Providence and God', 271; and Vlatko Vedral, 'Is the Universe Deterministic?' *New Scientist*, 50th Anniversary Special 1956–2006, 192/2578 (18 November 2006) 52–55.

45 Midgley, *Science and Poetry*, 166.

46 Dawkins, *The Selfish Gene*, 35.

47 Dawkins, *The Selfish Gene*, 60. See also Midgley, *Evolution as a Religion*, 145; and Midgley, *Science and Poetry*, 271.

88   CHAPTER 3

This vision, as we have seen, offers a bleak view of human life and freedom; free will is but an illusion, for the human self is but a site for competing gene cartels, which lead over time to the emergence of memes that become our minds and that exercise control over us in every respect. Lest it be thought that this is but an unfair representation of what Dawkins holds to be the case, the following is how he expresses it in his own words:

> Memes don't only leap from mind to mind by imitation, in culture. That is just the easily visible tip of the iceberg. They also thrive, multiply and compete within our minds. When we announce to the world a good idea, who knows what subconscious quasi-Darwinian selection has gone on behind the scenes inside our heads? Our minds are invaded by memes as ancient bacteria invaded our ancestors' cells and became mitochondria. Cheshire Cat-like, memes merge into our minds, even become our minds ...[48]

An intriguing aspect of this position is that Dawkins can hardly claim exemption from this process for himself, so that the views he expresses as his own in *The God Delusion* must ultimately derive from a sub-conscious process of 'quasi-Darwinian selection' that involves memes invading his mind 'Cheshire Cat-like', in order to control it at the behest of the underlying genes.[49] This position too belies his claim that scientific knowledge leads to 'exhilarating freedom' (362 [406]).[50] If anything, it evacuates the very notion of human freedom of any meaningful content; for the only freedom we can claim in this account of things – the *thought* that we are exhilaratingly free – is itself the product of an internal process over

48 Dawkins, *Unweaving the Rainbow*, 307. See also Midgley, *Science and Poetry*, 97; and Midgley, *Evolution as a Religion*, 53.
49 See the critiques of similar positions in Nichols, *The Sacred Cosmos*, 147–151, and Hick, *The New Frontier of Religion and Science*, 119–123.
50 It is noteworthy that in the course of his work Dawkins maintains focus on the power of human reason to the exclusion of any reflections on the human will. In a debate with David Quinn on *The Ryan Tubridy Show* on *RTE Radio* on the 9th October 2006, in the aftermath of the publication of *The God Delusion*, Dawkins conceded that 'free will is a very difficult philosophical question' and that 'I'm not interested in free will'. The transcript of the debate can be found in *The Irish Catholic* (Thursday, 4 January, 2007) 5–7.

which we have absolutely no control, dictated as it is by the running battles continually ongoing in our minds.

Having eliminated mind and purpose, together with spirit and freedom, from the nature of things, and having restricted them purely to the conscious realm as it has evolved over time, the pitfalls facing science-inspired humanity are many indeed. Though those like Dawkins who enthuse about this approach to life may be motivated by the highest ideals and be themselves full of purpose and meaning, their work ultimately denies those ideals enduring value by reducing them to the interaction of mindless, purposeless particles that are continuously active both within our minds and outside of them. Likewise, even though Dawkins claims that his use of the word 'selfish' is to be understood in a purely scientific sense, it has without doubt practical consequences in the moral sphere; he concedes, in fact, that 'gene selfishness will usually give rise to selfishness in individual behaviour',[51] and so 'we must even expect that children will deceive their parents, that husbands will cheat on wives, and that brother will lie to brother'.[52] Understood in these terms, ethics is finally reduced to a power struggle to the death, as selfish genes battle with one another for supremacy at the biological level and as equally competitive memes struggle for supremacy at the levels of human thought and culture.[53] In truth, the meme is an apt symbol for human culture and society as thus envisioned, where the human self, having been purged of its transcendent, spiritual dimension, has been reduced to the level of a semi-illusory epiphenomenon of materiality. As the end product of that thoroughly objectifying process, the meme – constituted as it is by a double 'me,' one immediately followed by another – literally and emphatically objectifies selfishness, enshrining it as the dominant characteristic of life in its entirety.

After the totalitarianism of the twentieth century, the inherent dangers of such a totalising, ideological stance to life ought to be abundantly clear. An ideology, to quote Arendt, 'is quite literally what its name

51   Dawkins, *The Selfish Gene*, 2.
52   Dawkins, *The Selfish Gene*, 65.
53   See Haught, *God after Darwin*, 124; Midgley, *Evolution as a Religion*, 150–153.

indicates: it is the logic of an idea'.[54] Applied to history, the ideological stance treats everything that occurs as simply the logical outworking in history of the idea in question: 'The ideology treats the course of events as though it followed the same "law" as the logical exposition of its "idea." ... The movement of history and the logical process of this notion are supposed to correspond to each other, so that whatever happens, happens according to the logic of one "idea."'[55] Likewise, when applied to society, the ideological stance is such that it attempts to seize control over every aspect of life, in the conviction that it alone can regulate society and lead people to fulfilment.[56]

In the work of Dawkins, the 'idea' which overrides all others is the 'selfish gene' and its logic is ruthlessly utilitarian, as he himself insists: '... Darwinian selection habitually targets and eliminates waste. Nature is a miserly accountant, grudging the pennies, watching the clock, punishing the smallest extravagance.... Nature cannot afford frivolous *jeux d'esprit*. Ruthless utilitarianism trumps, even if it doesn't always seem that way' (163 [190–191]). Hence, though it has not yet been pushed to the limit in any species, 'the logical conclusion to this trend ... would be for the genes to give the survival machine a single overall policy instruction: do whatever you think best to keep us alive'.[57]

This stance is thought provoking to say the least, but a simple question arises that cannot be avoided: is it true?

---

54 Arendt, *The Origins of Totalitarianism*, 604.
55 Arendt, *The Origins of Totalitarianism*, 604–605.
56 See Bob Goudzwaard, Mark Vander Vennen and David van Heemst, *Hope in Troubled Times: A New Vision for Confronting Global Crises* (Grand Rapids, Michigan: Baker Academic, 2007) 31–45, esp. 32–34.
57 Dawkins, *The Selfish Gene*, 60.

11. Broaching the Questions of Truth and Meaning

It actually does not require much effort to see that truth is among the casualties of the ruthless utilitarianism championed by Dawkins, as he spells out the implications of the position he advocates. In the strictly Darwinian account of things that he furnishes, truth, no less than freedom and many other issues, is finally to be judged by its utility in propagating the self-replicating gene, around which everything hinges. Once again, for Dawkins to claim exemption for his own extreme utilitarian stance on other grounds is not possible, since that very stance denies any independent, non-material, transcendent reference point for such grounds. As Thomas Crean observes, 'the materialistic Darwinism professed by our author is a self-refuting system'.[58] Though purporting to be truthful, such truth as his own work contains has merely utilitarian value; its contribution to truth lies not at any transcendent level, since as far as he is concerned that level does not exist independently of materiality, but simply in its usefulness in prolonging the lifespan of the particular genes of which he himself is the 'survival machine'. Two critical observations can be added immediately. First, the truth claims of Darwinian science over against religion furnished by Dawkins finally amount to no more than claims to be more ruthlessly utilitarian in genetic terms than religion. When seen in this light, it is highly improbable that any religious believers would be in any rush to dispute those claims. Second, the ruthless utilitarianism that underpins this approach constitutes a fertile breeding ground for the various 'isms' described above and a host of others, not least fatalism,[59] nihilism and totalitarianism.

As with the truth that is purely utilitarian, as with the altruism that is nobly undertaken for 'selfish' ends, and as with the purpose that ultimately has no rationale other than a limited decision-making value in certain life-threatening situations, so for the strict Darwinian the issue of

58 Crean, *A Catholic Replies to Professor Dawkins*, 117.
59 On science and fatalism, see Midgley, *Science and Poetry*, 137–145.

meaning itself is a biologically determined phenomenon that has validity only for the temporal duration of our conscious life on earth and to the extent we ourselves 'choose to make it' (360 [404]). There is, in these terms, no deeper meaning, beyond which science cannot probe, underlying the universe; it is finally absurd. The majority of scientists, according to Paul Davies, share similar views on the question of the meaning of the universe:

> The universe may or may not have a deep underlying unity, but there is no design, purpose or point to it all – at least none that would make sense to us. There is no God, no designer, no teleological principle, no destiny. Life in general, and human beings in particular, are an irrelevant embellishment in a vast and meaningless cosmos, the existence of which is an unfathomable mystery.[60]

Hence, as regards the question of its ultimate meaning, Davies considers 'the absurd universe' to be 'probably the majority position among scientists'.[61]

On the basis of the worldview that seems to have widespread consensus among scientists themselves, then, the all-embracing character and claims of scientific endeavours as they are now undertaken finally reduce the universe and the life it contains to meaningless absurdity. Yet a couple of questions immediately arise from the foregoing: is it the universe and life that are absurd, or is it the all-encompassing scientific claims that are absurd in reducing the universe and life to absurdity?

In seeking to provide an answer to those questions, it is worth recounting quite a different sort of testimony: the witness of Viktor Frankl to his experiences in a number of concentration camps, including Auschwitz, during the Second World War. Even in those camps, he testifies, where more than anywhere else in history our human capacity for evil was laid bare, where life was effectively reduced to nothing and where human depravity was witnessed on a daily basis, it was possible to find meaning

60 Davies, *The Goldilocks Enigma*, 295–296. See also Midgley, *Science and Poetry*, 137–169; and Haught, *Christianity and Science*, 60.
61 Davies, *The Goldilocks Enigma*, 295.

in the midst of utter meaninglessness: 'Fundamentally, therefore, any man can, even under such circumstances, decide what shall become of him – mentally and spiritually. He may retain his human dignity even in a concentration camp... It is this spiritual freedom – which cannot be taken away – that makes life meaningful and purposeful'.[62] That is the spiritual freedom defended by Christian faith too.

For the scientific worldview championed by Dawkins that claims privileged position as the ultimate arbiter of life's meaning, however, the notion of 'spiritual freedom' is simply another manifestation of the delusion that is 'God'. The cosmos which we inhabit is a meaninglessness place, and questions about it and about life that do not fall within the highly restrictive terms of reference deemed to be scientific are ultimately meaningless too. Yet, far from being adequate let alone comprehensive as an approach to the world and to life, this approach is incredibly naive in many respects, as a brief consideration of the question of meaning brings to the fore.

From Naive to Critical Realism

In addressing the ambiguity of realism, Bernard Lonergan contrasts the child's world of immediacy – the world of sense experience constituted by seeing and hearing, by touching and feeling, by smelling and tasting, by pleasure and pain and so forth – with the world mediated by meaning that emerges when a subject's intentional stance towards experience is considered and when questions of understanding and judgment are asked and answered.[63] As the human subject's command and use of language develop, a world of meaning opens up that enables her or him to draw on

---

62   Viktor E. Frankl, *Man's Search for Meaning: An Introduction to Logotherapy*, trans. Ilse Lasch (London: Hodder and Stoughton, 1964 [1962]) 66.

63   See Bernard Lonergan, *A Second Collection*, ed. William F. J. Ryan and Bernard J. Tyrrell (London: Darton, Longman & Todd, 1974) 241. See also Bernard Lonergan, *Method in Theology* (Toronto: University of Toronto Press, 1971) 76–77 and 238. A useful summary of Lonergan's position is provided by Fergus Kerr in *Twentieth-*

the riches of literature and philosophy, of science and religion, of theology and history, to adopt a conscious stance towards experience and towards life in all its profundity – not only present, but past and future too; not just actuality, but also possibility and probability; and not simply facts, but rights and duties too. It is important to emphasise that this world 'is not just given. Over and above what is given there is the universe that is intended by questions, that is organized by intelligence, that is described by language, that is enriched by tradition. It is an enormous world far beyond the comprehension of the nursery'.[64]

Lonergan goes on to explain that the world mediated by meaning is a fragile one for a variety of reasons: 'because meaning can go astray, because there is myth as well as science, fiction as well as fact, deceit as well as honesty, error as well as truth, that larger real world is insecure'.[65] Problems arise too when the world of immediacy is not properly distinguished from the world mediated by meaning; when that distinction is overlooked, 'an exceedingly stubborn and misleading myth'[66] arises that fundamentally distorts our stance towards the world. In this myth, knowing is equated simply with 'taking a good look; objectivity is a matter of seeing what is there to be seen; reality is whatever is given in immediate experience. Such is naive realism. Its offspring is empiricism'.[67] The empiricist, then, is one who takes naive realism seriously and proceeds to empty the world mediated by meaning of everything that is not given in immediate experience.[68]

Century Catholic Theologians: From Neoscholasticism to Nuptial Mysticism (Malden, MA, and Oxford, U.K.: Blackwell Publishing, 2006) 105–120.

64   Lonergan, *A Second Collection*, 241.
65   Lonergan, *Method in Theology*, 77.
66   Lonergan, *Method in Theology*, 238.
67   Lonergan, *A Second Collection*, 241. See also Lonergan, *Method in Theology*, 238.
68   Lonergan points out that the idealist, though accepting that knowing always includes understanding as well as sense, 'retains the empiricist's notion of reality, and so he thinks of the world mediated by meaning as not real but ideal'. Lonergan, *Method in Theology*, 238–239.

Adopting a stance that stands in sharp contrast to that of the naive realist, Lonergan argues for a critical realism that gives a central place to the self-transcendence of the human subject in the act of knowing.

> For the world mediated by meaning is a world known not by the sense experience of an individual but by the external and internal experience of a cultural community, and by the continuously checked and rechecked judgments of the community. Knowing, accordingly, is not just seeing; it is experiencing, understanding, judging, and believing. The criteria of objectivity are not just the criteria of ocular vision; they are the compounded criteria of experiencing, of understanding, of judging, and of believing. The reality known is not just looked at; it is given in experience, organized and extrapolated by understanding, posited by judgment and belief.[69]

In terms of this understanding, a truly objective stance towards the world in every field, in science as much as in theology, does not preclude authentic subjectivity but actually demands it, requiring attentiveness, intelligence, reasonableness and responsibility on the part of the human subject. In other words, 'genuine objectivity is the fruit of authentic subjectivity. It is to be attained only by attaining authentic subjectivity. To seek and employ some alternative prop or crutch invariably leads to some measure of reductionism'.[70]

As we have seen above, reductionism is rife today in science, the thrust of its whole approach suggesting that the ultimate answers to the questions that plague human existence can be found only in scientific labs amid the trails of debris, duly interpreted and explained by scientific reason, left in detection chambers by the most elusive particles, after less elusive ones have been accelerated to enormous speeds, crashed into one another and thus pulverised. From a Christian standpoint, though 'particle smashers' have a role to play, they are far too blunt and destructive a means to probe issues that are ultimately personal and spiritual and that have a meaning which is encapsulated in the question of God.

---

69   Lonergan, *Method in Theology*, 238.
70   Lonergan, *Method in Theology*, 292; see also 265.

The Question about God

Though the relationship between science and religious belief today is fraught with difficulties, those difficulties are no reason to abandon the dialogue and the search for mutual understanding. Though there may be religious believers who consider it 'a virtue to be satisfied with not understanding' (126 [152]), Christian faith from the very beginning has actively pursued such understanding and sought to give it coherent expression in its fidelity to the truth of Jesus Christ. Far from being content to wallow in ignorance, it no less than science seeks to come to a deeper understanding of the mystery of life and the intelligibility inherent in the universe; for the universe is an intelligible and meaningful place, a fact which requires coherent explanation. Once that is conceded, Bernard Lonergan argues, 'there arises the question whether the universe could be intelligible without having an intelligent ground. But that is the question about God'.[71]

Lonergan goes on to show that the same question arises through consideration of a whole series of further questions that are none too different from and no less difficult than the ones scattered throughout *The God Delusion.*

> Does there exist a reality that transcends the reality of this world? ... Has 'worth while' any ultimate meaning? ... But is the universe on our side, or are we just gamblers and, if we are gamblers, are we not perhaps fools, individually struggling for authenticity and collectively endeavoring to snatch progress from the ever mounting welter of decline? ... Does there or does there not necessarily exist a transcendent, intelligent ground of the universe? Is that ground or are we the primary instance of moral consciousness? Are cosmogenesis, biological evolution, and historical process basically cognate to us as moral beings or are they indifferent and so alien to us? Such is the question of God.[72]

---

71   Lonergan, *Method in Theology*, 101.
72   Lonergan, *Method in Theology*, 102–103.

The God question, he goes on to emphasise, is not 'a matter of image or feeling, of concept or judgment'[73] – and neither, we might add, is it a hypothesis – all of which pertain to answers; it is rather a question that arises out of the unrestricted conscious intentionality of human beings, in the measure that they advert to their own questioning and then 'proceed to question it.'[74] Within the horizon of human questioning and intentionality there lies a space for the divine, a shrine that cannot be ignored. 'The atheist may pronounce it empty. The agnostic may urge that he finds his investigation has been inconclusive. The contemporary humanist will refuse to allow the question to arise. But their negations presuppose the spark in our clod, our native orientation to the divine.'[75]

Notwithstanding the 'demolition job' attempted by Dawkins, then, the very stance he adopts and the questions he poses simply highlight the inescapability of the God question for human beings. The God question is inescapable, and the light it casts on the cosmos reveals it to be an inherently meaningful place. For Christian faith, Joseph Ratzinger reminds us, 'reality as a whole is a question pointing beyond itself'.[76] That question arises at every level of life in this world. It arises at the material level in the openness of materiality to non-materiality, manifestly evident in the extraordinary way the so-called 'mindless' universe has given rise not alone to life and mind, but to the realms of spirit and meaning too. It arises too at the level of scientific inquiry itself, which presupposes the patterned intelligibility of the world – the conditioning of matter by form, if one prefers the more traditional language – and seeks to ascertain the underlying reasons why. And, most critically, the question arises at the level of the human heart's characteristic orientation to the whole of reality that finds expression not only in unrestricted questioning but in an openness to love as the ground of intelligibility and meaning in the universe.

Materiality's inherent openness to non-materiality, to mind and to meaning cannot simply be reduced to a scientific question that denies

73 Lonergan, *Method in Theology*, 103.
74 Lonergan, *Method in Theology*, 103.
75 Lonergan, *Method in Theology*, 103.
76 Ratzinger, *In the Beginning*, 86.

entirely its transcendent reference. Indeed, far from eliminating the transcendent question, its denial, or the pretence that it does not arise, simply renders the question and how it is answered even more acute. The data furnished us by the sciences can be situated in a nihilistic framework that denies all ultimate values – a 'materialist quagmire',[77] to use the expression of John Haught – or that same data can be incorporated into a spiritual vision that celebrates the fullness of life and of all materiality in God. To express it in alternative terms, we can view the cosmos through a lens that ultimately reduces it to absurd meaninglessness, and pay the price such nihilism demands, or we can view the cosmos through a lens that sees it as intrinsically meaningful and purposeful, and seek to live accordingly. It is the latter option that Christians take, not on the basis of their own wishful thinking or foolhardy desires, but rather on the basis that the God question, which so preoccupies humankind, has its basis in a transcendent, spiritual, ultimately divine order that cannot be reduced to materiality.

In terms of the anthropological stance this position implies, the human person is a 'spirit in the world';[78] an embodied spirit who straddles the realms of spirit and matter in a manner that is characterised by mutuality, for the transcendent orientation of the former can be fulfilled only by ensuring the integrity of the latter, and vice versa. In terms of the stance towards the world this position implies, the universe and all that is in it have been brought into existence by God. Far from being merely an absurd hypothesis for which there is no evidence, then, the hallmark and imprint of the Creator – the 'fingerprints' of God, so to speak – can be detected everywhere in the natural world, most especially in the human spirit's intrinsic orientation to love and openness to the divine.

Christian faith goes even further, however, in suggesting that those characteristics are not simply open-ended and tenuous, delusory longings

---

77   Haught, *Christianity and Science*, 48.
78   The expression is Karl Rahner's, who develops a transcendental approach to the God
      question, though in a different manner to Bernard Lonergan. For a summary of his
      theological anthropology, see Stephen J. Duffy, *The Dynamics of Grace: Perspectives
      in Theological Anthropology* (Collegeville: Liturgical Press, 1993) 261–341.

of unfulfilled hearts that are evasive of reality and that constitute the root of most, if not all, of the troubles in the world. On the contrary, the human spirit's relationship to the transcendent is itself the mark of the divine in us, and that relationship has actually been brought to fulfilment in the most extraordinary way, not by our own endeavours but by the coming of God into our world in Jesus Christ. In him, by means of his life, death and resurrection, the ultimate meaning of our world is disclosed and its transformation definitively assured.

As the first part of this work comes to a close and as the second part beckons, then, the need to explore the above claims in the light of Christian faith has become clear. That exploration will take place over three chapters, dealing, in very broad terms, with the themes of creation, redemption and revelation. In the fourth chapter, a brief outline of the Christian theology of creation, into which scientific data can be meaningfully and holistically incorporated, is presented. The following chapter will look more closely at how human freedom and evil in the world are intertwined, with a view to showing how redemption in Jesus Christ opens a path by which the authentic religious impulse of humanity can be perfected and all its distorted manifestations, not least the pseudo-scientific ones examined in this and the preceding chapters, overcome. Then, in the final chapter, the attempt will be made to draw things together by reflecting on our blindness to the presence of God revealed in and through Jesus Christ: a blindness that is finally traceable to the voluntary self-effacement of God, whose power does not overwhelm us but rather becomes manifest in the weakness of the crucified love that envelops the world and that never ceases to call forth a free response on the part of all human beings in their creaturely freedom.

PART II

The Foolishness of Divine Love

*For since, in the wisdom of God, the world did not know
God through wisdom, God decided, through the foolishness
of our proclamation, to save those who believe.... For God's
foolishness is wiser than human wisdom, and God's weakness is stronger than human strength.*

I CORINTHIANS 1:21, 25

CHAPTER 4

The Trinitarian Grammar of Creation

Science is supposed to be the pursuit of truth, but in secular cultures it has become the chief vehicle for myth. The human needs that were once expressed in religion have not disappeared. From the cult of cryogenics to absurd neo-Darwinian ideas, the core myths of western religion are being recycled as science. In the course of this transformation, the wisdom they contain is being lost.
— JOHN GRAY[1]

Everything may thus be a quantum fluctuation out of nothing.
— FRANK CLOSE[2]

Evolution, then, is the creation myth of our age.
— MARY MIDGLEY[3]

'A thirst for explanation, for causality', writes George Steiner, 'inhabits our nature. We do want to know: why?'[4] Though the beginning itself lies beyond our grasp, he goes on to point out, by means of the tools fashioned by human ingenuity and through the information gained by their use, 'late twentieth-century science is now "within three seconds" of

---

1   John Gray, *Heresies: Against Progress and Other Illusions* (London: Granta Books, 2004) 65.
2   Frank Close, *The Void* (Oxford and New York: Oxford University Press, 2007) 156.
3   Midgley, *Evolution as a Religion*, 33.
4   Steiner, *Grammars of Creation*, 2.

the start of this universe. The creation story can be told as never before.[5] It can be told in the language of mathematics and physics, by means of esoteric symbols and equations that display an incredible coherence and symmetry and even beauty to those in the know. Yet therein lies a problem, for those experts 'in the know' are few and, overbearing in their own knowledge, most of them are more than content to leave the 'why' question unanswered, if not to dismiss it altogether as Dawkins does (see 56 [80]). That is hardly surprising, given that this question, along with numerous other questions around purpose and meaning and hope, lies outside the highly restricted scope of scientific language, and so is incapable of being expressed in purely that language.

Yet there is another way of telling the story of origins, a far older and more symbolic way of narrating it that takes a risk on transcendence, on the openness of the material to the spiritual and on the underlying presence of God, while drawing on the richness of art and poetry and music to communicate that risk. Again, as Steiner observes, 'the arts glory in creation, in creativity'.[6] An artistic approach of this kind gives centre stage to purpose and meaning and hope, inviting participation and calling for a response. Steiner's own wager 'supposes a passage ... from meaning to meaningfulness. The conjecture is that "God" *is*, not because our grammar is outworn; but that grammar lives and generates worlds because there is the wager on God'.[7] Far from being a purely material reality, devoid of meaning and purpose apart from that conferred by human beings in their attempts to manipulate it, the world in this perspective is an extraordinarily beautiful, meaningful and purposeful reality; an artistic reality even, which can be described and spoken of because 'the covenant

---

5   Steiner, *Grammars of Creation*, 10. The figure of 'three seconds' is already out of date. It seems that scientists working at the Large Hadron Collider, opened during September 2008 at CERN, near Geneva, aim to achieve a glimpse of how things were within a tiny fraction of a second of the start of the universe.
6   Steiner, *Grammars of Creation*, 23.
7   George Steiner, *Real Presences* (Chicago: University of Chicago Press, London: Faber and Faber, 1989) 4. For further reflections on the topic of creativity, see Beattie, *The New Atheists*, 154–176.

between word and object' allows that 'the raw material of existentiality has its analogue in the structure of narrative'.[8]

The covenant between word and world of which Steiner speaks is traceable for the Christian, and for the Jew, back to the dawn of time, to the event of creation itself. In that extraordinary event of which the Scriptures speak, the beauty, meaning and purpose that inhere in the world are firmly rooted in the gift of the divine Artist, communicated initially at the moment of creation and continuing to underpin its existence at each moment as time and space evolve. Though mathematical calculation and scientific endeavours greatly help us to appreciate, understand and render precise the dynamics of those processes, the basic conviction and vision are rooted in faith and they are best understood in the language of symbol and poetry that abounds in the Scriptures and in the life of the Church.

I. God's Word and World

For the inspired writers of the Hebrew Scriptures, the universe and all that is in it enjoy a special status as works of God, whose creative activity is multifaceted and open to being described by a huge variety of images and symbols: among them, for example, God as divine artisan, the maker of heaven and earth (Is 37:16), and God as the potter who moulds human beings out of the dust of the earth (Is 45:9).[9] Of special importance among the various approaches is the one furnished by the opening chapter of the book of Genesis, creation by the divine word.

---

8   Steiner, *Real Presences*, 90. See also Steiner, *Grammars of Creation*, 127, 219 and 228.

9   For a comprehensive analysis and further examples, see Terence E. Fretheim, *God and the World in the Old Testament: A Relational Theology of Creation* (Nashville: Abingdon Press, 2005) 1–48.

Creation as Event: The Divine Speech Act

'In the Hebraic perspective', Steiner observes, 'creation is a rhetoric, a literal speech act... The making of being is a saying. The *ruah Elohim*, the breath or *pneuma* of the Creator speaks the world'.[10] As Genesis 1 makes very clear, creation can be understood as a series of utterances spoken by God that are powerful, formative and definitive. That divine speech act is powerful, for it effects what it speaks: 'Let there be ... And it was so'. That divine speech act is formative too, for it differentiates Creator from all that is created and establishes an unfathomable distance between them, bridgeable only by the divine power; it 'maps' the world, so to speak, demarcating boundaries and establishing limits, imposing order and shape, and giving form and consistency to the hitherto 'formless void' (Gen 1:1) that simply was at the beginning; and it separates created realities among themselves – light from darkness, waters under the firmament from those above and those below, and so on.[11] Far from being accidental or incidental, that speech act is definitive, for in a quite deliberate, intentional and purposeful fashion, it signals the divine commitment to the created order called into existence and standing in an ongoing relationship with the Creator.

The Genesis story makes very clear that creation involves more than simply the 'one-off' event at the beginning, completed and perfected in the seven-day time frame around which the story is symbolically structured, in a manner not to be understood as a literal description of what occurred. On the contrary, the story is laden with covenantal symbolism. As Joseph Ratzinger reminds us, for example, the number seven symbolises

10   Steiner, *Grammars of Creation*, 27–28.
11   See Mackey, *Christianity and Creation*, 30–33. See also André LaCoque, 'Cracks in the Wall', in *Thinking Biblically: Exegetical and Hermeneutical Studies*, by André LaCoque and Paul Ricoeur, trans. David Pellauer (Chicago and London: University of Chicago Press, 1998) 3–29; and, in the same volume, Paul Ricoeur, 'Thinking Creation', 31–67.

in a most profound way creation's 'Sabbath structure'[12] and its fundamental orientation to worship. The repetition of the phrase, 'God said',
ten times in the creation account is no less significant, for in pointing to
God's later giving of the Ten Commandments, it offers 'a translation of the
language of the universe, a translation of God's logic, which constructed
the universe'.[13] At the heart of that logic is the dynamic relationship of
God with creation that comes clearly to the fore in human beings.

Creation, as depicted by Genesis, is an ongoing, dynamic process in
which the created realities themselves have a constructive role to play as
integral to the divine intention. Far from being a unilateral imposition,
then, God's commitment to creation is such that it not only leaves room
for a creaturely response but it is actually incomplete until that response
is forthcoming. Terence Fretheim observes that the divine speaking is
such that the recipient of the word has an important role to play in the
shaping of the created order. 'Such a perspective indicates that creation
in Genesis 1 is seen in terms of process and not simply as punctiliar event,
for temporal space is given for response'.[14] The divine speech act is evoca-
tive, then, climaxing in the blessing that empowers humans who have
been created in the divine image and likeness (Gen 1:27) to creativity in
imitation of their Creator: 'Be fruitful and multiply, and fill the earth
and subdue it ...' (Gen 1:28).[15] The divine creativity also endows human
beings with the power of naming, an extraordinarily creative power that
defines their position and role in relation to every other creature (Gen
2:19–20). In response to the divine initiative, then, there arises a corresponding creaturely one that renders human beings uniquely creative in
their own right and uniquely capable of entering a relationship of dia-

---

12   Ratzinger, *In the Beginning*, 30. See also Fretheim, *God and the World in the Old
     Testament*, 61–64 and 144–145. For a general overview of the theology of creation
     from biblical times to the present day, see José Morales, *Creation Theology* (Dublin
     and Portand, OR: Four Courts Press, 2001).
13   Ratzinger, *In the Beginning*, 26.
14   Fretheim, *God and the World in the Old Testament*, 38.
15   See Fretheim, *God and the World in the Old Testament*, 49; also LaCoque, 'Cracks
     in the Wall', 10.

logue with God. That capacity and creativity are ultimately defining of the human person.[16]

The God of Genesis far transcends the created realm and, hence, is an unfathomable mystery to the human creature, who is puny by comparison. Nevertheless, God is not remote or distant, but continues to be intimately involved in the creative process, which is ongoing. The text makes clear that God's involvement extends beyond speaking and acting to evaluating and experiencing the fruits of the divine labours. That is particularly evident in the divine judgment that the created realities are good, or, indeed, 'not good' (Gen 2:18) and requiring further divine activity, as the case may be. The message is thus conveyed that the Creator continues to interact with the creation, in a relationship that is quite affective. Fretheim puts it like this: 'In evaluating, God sees, indeed *experiences*, that which has been created and is *affected* by what is seen, thereby revealing an *ongoing* relationship of consequence with that which has been created'.[17] Creation, in other words, involves a dynamic interrelationship between Creator and creature, the comprehensive nature of which is drawn out in other books of the Hebrew Scriptures.

A Relational God and a Relational World

God's presence in the created order is universal, filling and underpinning that order, which never ceases to tell of the divine glory: 'The heavens are telling the glory of God; and the firmament proclaims his handiwork' (Ps 19:1; see also Ps 148 and Jer 23:24). Yet God's presence in the created world is such that it frequently passes unnoticed and goes unrecognised, even by believers. For the character of the relationship freely set in place by God at creation, involving respect for the integrity of creatures, is underpinned by a voluntary self-limitation in the exercise of divine power. Hence, though the relationship between God and human creatures is very much

16   See Ratzinger, *In the Beginning*, 47–48.
17   Fretheim, *God and the World in the Old Testament*, 40.

an asymmetrical one, the creature made of dust being quite puny and insignificant in comparison to the Creator, creation as a divine project involves an extraordinary self-restraint on God's part in all subsequent dealings with creatures. Having freely created human beings in the divine image and likeness and endowed them with freedom, the eternal Creator thereafter freely assumes the burden of that freedom in engaging with them. Hence, as Fretheim remarks, 'God so enters into relationships that the human will can stand over against the will of God ... The divine will is resistable; God does not always get God's will done in the world, most especially because of continuing human resistance'.[18] To that resistance ultimately can be traced the evil that marks so much of life in the world.

As with the limitation on divine action with respect to human freedom, so also there is limitation on divine action with respect to time. Having taken time to create the world and created the world in time, the eternal Creator thereafter freely assumes the burden and constraints of time in further engaging with it in historical terms. Though the Scriptural authors had no inkling whatever of the enormity of what that involved in purely temporal terms, we now know from scientific evidence that those constraints extended over billions of years, as life evolved and the world took shape. Yet, while the knowledge we have gained of the various scientific processes involved in those developments furnishes us with remarkable new insights, it does not alter the fundamental Scriptural insight that the created world in its entirety originated in God who remains deeply committed to it. That commitment involves varying intensifications of the divine presence and commitment, until they come to historical fruition in the call of Abraham and the formation of Israel as a people.

Israel's existence as a people was decisively linked with the liberating event of the Exodus, during which the personal character of God – 'I am who I am' – was revealed to Moses in the incident at the burning bush on Mount Horeb, described in Exodus 3:1–15. Though utterly transcendent to the world, mysterious and hidden and infinitely distant from creatures, God paradoxically remains active in the world, intervening historically

18   Fretheim, *God and the World in the Old Testament*, 22.

to redeem Israel and to enter freely into a covenant relationship with it
as a partner. That covenant sets the benchmark for Israel's understanding of God and of God's redemptive activity on its behalf, which is not
exclusive but is oriented to the entire creation.[19]

The prophets are the great interpreters of God's covenant relationship
with Israel. Isaiah, for example, expounds the grammar of the covenant
in several noteworthy passages, linking it inextricably with the ongoing
creativity of God in history.

> Thus says God, the Lord,
> who created the heavens and stretched them out,
> who spread out the earth and what comes from it,
> who gives breath to the people upon it
> and spirit to those who walk in it:
> I am the Lord, I have called you in righteousness,
> I have taken you by the hand and kept you;
> I have given you as a covenant to the people,
> a light to the nations ... (Is 42:5–6).

> But now thus says the Lord,
> he who created you, O Jacob,
> he who formed you, O Israel:
> Do not fear, for I have redeemed you;
> I have called you by name, you are mine (Is 43:1).

> Thus says the Lord, your Redeemer,
> who formed you in the womb:
> I am the Lord, who made all things,
> who alone stretched out the heavens,
> who by myself spread out the earth (Is. 44:24).

19 See Fretheim, *God and the World in the Old Testament*, 110. The significance of
this ought not be underestimated. George Steiner finds direct links between the
'I am' of the burning bush and 'the presumptions of concordance, of equivalence,
of translatability which, though imperfect, empower our dictionaries, our syntax,
our rhetoric. That "I am" has, as it were, at an overwhelming distance, informed all
predication'. Steiner, *Grammars of Creation*, 239–240. The presumptions underpinning the 'theory of everything', already critiqued in a previous chapter, can be
traced to this point too.

> Listen to me, O Jacob, and Israel, whom I called:
> I am He; I am the first, and I am the last.
> My hand laid the foundation of the earth,
> and my right hand spread out the heavens;
> when I summon them, they stand at attention (Is 48:12–13).

For Isaiah and for the other prophets too, covenant and creation go hand in hand, mutually interpreting one another in bearing witness to the abiding presence and activity of God in the world and in history. God's redemptive activity on behalf of Israel stands in fundamental continuity with God's purposes for the created order; for both are oriented to the new creation, the 'new heavens and new earth' (see Is 65:17), that God is bringing into existence to fulfil the divine purposes for the world.[20]

Creation emerges as a key motif too in the Wisdom literature, the various texts of which spell out the depth of the wisdom that inheres in the world and that grounds its beauty, its order and its purpose. Strikingly imaged in feminine terms throughout this literature (see, for example, Wis 7:22–30), personified wisdom was the first of God's created works, an all-pervading presence at God's side in every subsequent creative act (see Prov 8:22–31).[21] The wisdom that God poured out on all created realities underpins nature and is discernible to the one who is open to all things divine: 'For from the greatness and beauty of created things comes a corresponding perception of their Creator' (Wis 13:5). For the believer, then, knowledge of God brings a true understanding of all created things in their relatedness and interconnectedness.

> For both we and our words are in his hand,
> as are all understanding and skill in crafts.
> For it is he who gave me unerring knowledge of what exists,
> to know the structure of the world and the activity of the elements;
> the beginning and end and middle of times,
> the alterations of the solstices and the changes of the seasons,
> the cycles of the year and the constellations of the stars,

---

20   See Fretheim, *God and the World in the Old Testament*, 181–198.
21   For an analysis of this and related passages, see Fretheim, *God and the World in the Old Testament*, 205–218.

the natures of animals and the tempers of wild animals,
the powers of spirits and the thoughts of human beings,
the varieties of plants and the virtues of roots;
I learned both what is secret and what is manifest,
for wisdom, the fashioner of all things, taught me (Wis 7:16–22).

It is clear from this that a truly wise stance towards the created world is grounded in a faith relationship with God. Incredibly, however, such is human folly that those who are ignorant of God fail to make the connection and to discern the Creator in the divine handiwork.

For all people who were ignorant of God were foolish by nature;
and they were unable from the good things that are seen
to know the one who exists,
nor did they recognize the artisan while paying heed to his works;
but they supposed that either fire or wind or swift air,
or the circle of the stars, or turbulent water,
or the luminaries of heaven were the gods that rule the world...
For from the greatness and beauty of created things
comes a corresponding perception of their Creator.
Yet these people are little to be blamed,
for perhaps they go astray
while seeking God and desiring to find him.
For while they live among his works, they keep searching,
and they trust in what they see,
because the things that are seen are beautiful... (Wis 13:1,5–7).

Though the author of these passages knew nothing about the all-explanatory scientific views associated with genes and memes, the same words are no less applicable in that context too.

In sum, the Old Testament presents a view of reality as the handiwork of God in a manner that puts relationality between God and creatures centre stage. We live in a world created by God, who remains committed to it and who continues to relate to it in a way that is creative and faithful, and that is life-enhancing and life-fulfilling for every creature. Notwithstanding the widespread breakdown in relationships that occurred, traceable fundamentally to the failure of human creatures to respond appropriately to the divine initiatives, God's intention is not to discard creation but to renew it through and through, by means of the historical choice of Israel as the covenant people. Creation, then, is open to completion and, as such, it is oriented to the future. For the Christian, that fulfilment has already been accomplished in Jesus Christ.

The Christ Event: Incarnate Word and Wisdom of God

In words of extraordinary profundity and insight that echo the opening verse of the book of Genesis, the Gospel of John begins by expounding the mystery of divine Incarnation in human flesh in Jesus Christ.

> In the beginning was the Word,
> and the Word was with God,
> and the Word was God.
> He was in the beginning with God.
> All things came into being through him,
> and without him not one thing came into being.
> What has come into being in him was life,
> and the life was the light of all people.
> The light shines in the darkness,
> and the darkness did not overcome it (Jn 1:1–5).

Continuing in the same vein, John draws both on Jewish and Greek religious traditions, while going far beyond them to convey the divine status and identity of Jesus Christ, as the Word and Wisdom of God become incarnate. Jesus Christ, in other words, is the primordial divine utterance, intrinsic to the very self-definition of the monotheistic God of Israel. All that subsequently happens in the course of Jesus' ministry, death and resurrection, as recounted in the Gospel, has to be understood in this light, for the Incarnation itself constitutes God's supreme act of love for the world: 'For God so loved the world that he gave his only Son, so that everyone who believes in him may not perish but may have eternal life' (Jn 3:16). Everything done and undergone by Jesus Christ in the course of his earthly life thus begins with a descent into this world from the Father, and it ends with his return to the Father to share once more the glory that was his even before the foundation of the world. It is within the framework of abiding love that creation has to be situated and understood.

The christocentric thrust of John's theology is reinforced by that of Paul, who in addressing the Areopagus in Athens points them to the God in whom 'we live and move and have our being' (Acts 17:28). In developing this theme in his own writings, Paul underscores the pre-existence of Christ and his role in bringing creation about. In the striking opening passage of his letter to the Ephesians, for example, he paints a vast canvas that encompasses the entire universe, as he details how God has chosen us in Christ 'before the foundation of the world to be holy and blameless before him in love' (Eph 1:4). God's mysterious intent in lavishing divine love upon us in Christ, Paul goes on to affirm, constitutes the divine plan 'for the fullness of time, to gather up all things in him, things in heaven and things on earth' (Eph 1:9–10). The same themes are expressed even more strikingly in the famous hymn found in the opening chapter of the letter to the Colossians.

> He is the image of the invisible God,
> the firstborn of all creation;
> for in him all things in heaven and on earth were created,
> things visible and invisible,
> whether thrones or dominations or rulers or powers –
> all things have been created through him and for him.
> He himself is before all things, and in him all things hold together.
> He is the head of the body, the church;
> he is the beginning, the firstborn from the dead,
> so that he might come to have first place in everything.
> For in him all the fullness of God was pleased to dwell,
> and through him God was pleased to reconcile to himself all things,
> whether on earth or in heaven,
> by making peace through the blood of his cross (Col 1:15–20).

Paul thus underscores both the origin and finality of creation in Christ, whose death and resurrection not only reveal the true nature of our creaturely status before God but actually bring it, along with the entire cosmos, to completion and perfection as a 'new creation' (see 2 Cor 5:17; Gal 6:15;

and Eph 2:15). In the language of the letter to the Romans, creation is groaning with eager longing while it awaits liberation from its bondage to decay and a share in the glorious destiny of the children of God, effected by Christ and communicated by his Spirit (see Rom 8:18–25).

For those who take the New Testament as their guide, Jesus Christ is both the first and the final utterance of God. Manifest in human form, he is complete and perfect in every way, the fullness of what God has to communicate to us. He is God's definitive self-expression, the one in whom every preceding utterance of God, including creation itself, is situated in a definitive interpretative context, on the one hand, and perfected, on the other. He is, finally, the exegete and interpreter of creation par excellence, unfolding its grammar and constituting its goal as he brings it to salvation and makes it new.

Creatio ex nihilo

In the Patristic period of the Church, reflection by believers on the mysteries of faith found in the New Testament continued apace. For our purposes here, the development of three key doctrines, the Trinity, the Incarnation and *creatio ex nihilo*, is of immense importance.

The doctrine of the Trinity is decisive because it clarifies the fundamental Christian understanding of God as Triune, one God in three persons, Father, Son and Holy Spirit. In the face of numerous other understandings that had come to the fore between the first and the fourth centuries, all of them subsequently deemed to be heterodox, the Church at the Councils of Nicaea (325) and Constantinople I (381) outlined the creed that constitutes the benchmark of Trinitarian orthodoxy. In terms of this understanding, God is wholly and essentially relational, for the Father, Son and Holy Spirit, who are truly distinct, share the one divine nature and cannot be conceived apart from their relationships with one another. In alternative terms, God is wholly and essentially one, constituted as such by the infinite communion of equality and love that pertains to the Father, Son and Holy Spirit in the mutual relationships that uniquely distinguish them: the Father as the unbegotten one, the Son

as begotten by the Father (generation), and the Holy Spirit as proceed-
ing from the Father and the Son (procession). Christian theology thus
emphasises the category of relationality as the key to understanding the
mystery of God: as a Trinity of persons who are mutually constitutive
of and infinitely communing with one another, God is constituted and
defined by relationality.[22]

The doctrine of *creatio ex nihilo* is no less important for the Christian
understanding of the world, because it decisively refutes other conceptions that are fundamentally at odds with the mystery of Jesus Christ.
Among such conceptions prevalent during the patristic period when the
doctrine was formulated, for example, was the radically dualist Gnostic
one that viewed the material world as irredeemably evil, the product of an
evil being or 'demiurge' that stands in opposition to the God who reigns
supreme over the spiritual realm and who imparts the knowledge (*gnosis*)
that constitutes salvation. Likewise, in opposition to and in refutation of
conventional Greek philosophical wisdom that nothing could arise from
nothing and that the world was eternal, early Christian believers defended
the integrity of creation as an entirely gratuitous achievement of God,
acting simply out of goodness and without preconditions. Drawing on
the text of 2 Maccabees 7:28 – 'I beg you, my child, to look at the heaven
and the earth and see everything that is in them, and recognize that God
did not make them out of things that existed' – they broke through the
conceptual straitjacket of Greek thought to develop the radical teaching that God created the world 'out of nothing'.[23] In the words of St
Augustine,

22   Clear explanations of the process of development of Trinitarian doctrine can
     be found in several books: for example, Gerald O'Collins, *The Tripersonal God:
     Understanding and Interpreting the Trinity* (London: Geoffrey Chapman, 1999);
     and Thomas Marsh, *The Triune God: A Biblical, Historical and Theological Study*
     (Dublin: The Columba Press, 1994).
23   For overviews of these issues, see Morales, *Creation Theology*, 41–52; Kelly, *An
     Expanding Theology*, 91–126; Zachary Hayes, *The Gift of Being: A Theology of
     Creation* (Collegeville: Liturgical Press, 2001) 41–45; Ormerod, *Creation, Grace,
     and Redemption*, 1–10; and Leo Scheffczyk, *Creation and Providence*, trans.

In the beginning, that is from yourself, in your wisdom which is begotten of your substance, you made something and made it out of nothing.... It cannot possibly be right for anything which is not of you to be equal to you. Moreover, there was nothing apart from you out of which you could make them, God one in three and three in one. That is why you made heaven and earth out of nothing, a great thing and a little thing, since you, both omnipotent and good, make all things good, a great heaven and a little earth. You were, the rest was nothing. Out of nothing you made heaven and earth, two entities, one close to you, the other close to being nothing; the one to which only you are superior, the other to which what is inferior is nothingness.[24]

Against this background, the doctrine of the Incarnation – solemnly defined in terms of the hypostatic, personal union of two natures, divine and human, in Jesus Christ by the Council of Chalcedon in 451 – constitutes a decisive affirmation of the Christian understanding of reality. Not only is matter good, but it is the handwork of the Triune God, its Creator, and it has already been perfected spiritually in God's redemptive act of uniting divine and human in Jesus Christ.[25]

Early Christian thinkers were quite clear that creation is good and beautiful and that it bears the hallmarks of its Triune Creator, vestiges of whom can be found everywhere in it. Most especially, they can be found in human beings, who are created in the divine image and likeness, and particularly in their acts of knowing and loving. According to St Augustine, for instance, human love involves a lover, a beloved and the act of love itself. 'Now love means someone loving and something loved with love. There you are with three, the lover, what is being loved,

---

Richard Strachan (New York: Herder and Herder, London: Burns & Oates, 1970) 47–112.

24 St Augustine, *Confessions*, trans. Henry Chadwick (Oxford and New York: Oxford University Press, 1992) Book XII.vii (7), 249.

25 See Frances Young, 'Christology and Creation: Towards an Hermeneutic of Patristic Christology', in T. Merrigan and J. Haers (eds), *The Myriad Christ: Plurality and the Quest for Unity in Contemporary Christology* (Leuven: Leuven University Press, 2000) 191–205.

and love'.[26] The human mind constitutes an even more persuasive image of the Trinity for Augustine, in that the mind's activity involves presence to itself (self-presence), knowledge of itself (self-knowledge) and love for itself (self-love). A further refinement of this psychological scheme into the pattern of memory, intelligence and willing, opens up a quite insightful way of looking at the relationships of the Three in God. Though obviously the analogies falter, offering us at best a pale reflection of the unity and distinctions that exist in God, their value lies in pointing to the reasonableness of Trinitarian belief and in expressing it in an intelligible way.[27]

Augustine's approach to theology proved to be hugely influential in the Western tradition, which reached a highpoint in the synthesis developed by Thomas Aquinas in the Middle Ages. Thomas conceives creation in terms of a great circular movement of 'exit' and 'return': everything comes from God ('the One who is', the transcendent origin who is above and beyond all things) and is patterned on Jesus Christ (who is the exemplar of all created things) by a free creative act that inaugurates time and brings the universe into existence; and, through the humanity and salvific work of Jesus Christ, everything ultimately returns to God, who is also their final end.[28] In this light, there is clearly a very intimate relationship between Creator and creature and between Redeemer and redeemed: to be created is to bear a certain likeness to God – an orientation or movement underpinned by God's ongoing presence and activity, yet that truly pertains to the creature at its own natural level and that tends towards ever greater participation in God; while to be redeemed is for the creature, through the grace of the Redeemer, to achieve its ultimate end in the beatific vision by participating in the divine nature,

26   St Augustine, *The Trinity*, trans. Edmund Hill, ed. John E. Rotelle (Brooklyn, New York: New City Press, 1991) Book VIII.14, 255.
27   For overviews of Augustine's trinitarian theology and some references, see O'Collins, *The Tripersonal God*, 135–141; and Marsh, *The Triune God*, 131–137.
28   See Kerr, *After Aquinas*, 73–96.

in the eternal communion of Father, Son and Holy Spirit.[29] Thomas, it has to be insisted, recognised clearly the impossibility of furnishing proofs for any of this in the strict sense, apart from faith. That recognition, however, does not render the human mind totally impotent in the face of a mystery that is at once utterly simple (because God's essence is to exist, which is not true of creatures because the fact of their existence is clearly distinguishable from what they exist as)[30] and quite impenetrable (because God's plenitude utterly surpasses our limited capacity to grasp). On the contrary, given the traces of the divine in creation and starting from the way the world is, the mind's resources can be employed to investigate the mystery and thereby to develop reasonable arguments that God exists as the intelligible ground of reality.[31] Arguments for the existence of God can thus be presented that invoke causality (arguing from the changeable and defective to the unchangeable and perfect), eminence (involving recognition of God as possessing in a pre-eminent, completely perfect, way everything of the good that is in the world) and negation (accepting that the divine perfections are so utterly beyond us that we ultimately know God, even in the beatific vision, only as infinitely surpassing us and thus finally as unknown).[32]

---

29   See Robert Barron, *Thomas Aquinas: Spiritual Master* (New York: Crossroad, 1996) 109–139; and Torrell, *Saint Thomas Aquinas*, Vol. 2, *Spiritual Master*, 40–42. See also Anselm K. Min, *Paths to the Triune God: An Encounter between Aquinas and Recent Theologies* (Notre Dame: University of Notre Dame Press, 2005) esp. 12–50.

30   See Eleonore Stump, *Aquinas* (London and New York: Routledge, 2003) 92–130, esp. 97; and David B. Burrell, 'Act of Creation with Its Theological Consequences', in Thomas Weinandy, Daniel Keating and John Yocum (eds), *Aquinas on Doctrine: A Critical Introduction* (London and New York: T & T Clark, 2004) 27–44, esp. 29.

31   See Burrell, 'Act of Creation with Its Theological Consequences', 38.

32   See Torrell, *Saint Thomas Aquinas*, 40–42; Min, *Paths to the Triune God*, 150–153; Kerr, *After Aquinas*, 52–72; and Kelly, *An Expanding Theology*, 99–105. Keith Ward seeks to reformulate the traditional proofs in line with contemporary scientific thought in his work, *Why There Almost Certainly Is a God*, 102–123.

'For High Scholasticism', Hans Urs von Balthasar writes, 'creation is embraced within the Trinity, which is its inalienable precondition. "The possibility of creation rests in the reality of the Trinity. A non-trinitarian God could not be the Creator.""[33] It was precisely that conviction which underpinned subsequent scientific exploration of the natural world by Christian believers, who viewed the regularities and patterns of nature as reflecting the mind of its Creator. Their desacralising of the cosmos in this manner and their probing and articulation of 'the laws of nature' on this basis thus played no small part in the development of the scientific enterprise as we know it today.[34]

II. Situating Science in a Framework of Divine Love

With the rapid development of scientific knowledge in the modern period and with a whole series of discoveries challenging and undermining the traditional worldview, the medieval synthesis fragmented, to be replaced over the course of several centuries by the critical scientific outlook that holds sway in Western discourse to this day. That outlook in the form presented by its most vocal adherents, as we have seen, has no place for religious faith, which is viewed as an exercise in irrationality that, though benign in some respects, is past its 'sell-by' date and is best dismissed entirely because of its disastrous consequences.

It is abundantly clear from our vantage point today that the medieval synthesis cannot be put back together again; and that, indeed, any attempt to roll the clock back in that direction is an exercise in folly, akin

33   Hans Urs von Balthasar, *Theo-Drama: Theological Dramatic Theory*, Vol. V, *The Last Act*, trans. Graham Harrison (San Francisco: Ignatius Press, 1998) 61.
34   See Alister McGrath, *A Scientific Theology*, I, 225–232; Alister McGrath, *A Scientific Theology*, Vol. II, *Reality* (Edinburgh and New York: T & T Clark, 2002) 153–154; and Enrique Dussel, *History and the Theology of Liberation: A Latin American Perspective*, trans. John Drury (Maryknoll, New York: Orbis Books, 1976) 69.

to attempting to put 'Humpty Dumpty' together again after his fall. The challenge instead is to forge a new synthesis that integrates contemporary scientific knowledge with Christian truth.[35] Such a task is next to impossible at the present moment, given the forward march of science that continues apace and that, as Dawkins's work makes clear, is intent on explaining everything in a purely naturalistic, mechanistic way. Yet there are some grounds for optimism too, for contrary to the monism advocated by Dawkins that reduces every dimension of life to the material, physics more than ever understands the universe in dynamic, interconnected and relational terms. For example, in relation to particles at the quantum level, Mary Midgley observes that 'scientists no longer think in terms of hard, separate, unchangeable atoms at all but of particles that are essentially interconnected'.[36] In this perspective, the fundamental 'stuff' of the universe is nothing other than a dynamic series or network of interrelated events and overlapping fields, not a conglomeration of discrete, self-enclosed, irreducible, fully isolated and fully isolatable, identical pieces of solid matter. As such, reality is fundamentally relational, with every entity constituting it existing in relation to other entities and none of them standing isolated and alone.[37]

From a Christian perspective, as Wolfhart Pannenberg maintains, it is abundantly clear that 'if theologians want to conceive of God as the creator of the real world, they cannot possibly bypass the scientific description of that world'.[38] At the same time, the Christ event is utterly

35 For insightful remarks on the topic, see Ormerod, *Creation, Grace, and Redemption*, 23–45; and Kelly, *An Expanding Theology*, 91–124.

36 Midgley, *Science and Poetry*, 82; see also 11; Mackey, *Christianity and Creation*, 54–55; and Polkinghorne, *Science and the Trinity*, 73–75.

37 See Pannenberg, *Toward a Theology of Nature*, 20, 23–24; also Polanyi, *Personal Knowledge*, 398–405. For approaches that are more 'new age' in orientation, see Fritjof Capra, *The Turning Point: Science, Society, and the Rising Culture* (Toronto: Bantam Books, 1982) esp. 87, 265–304; and Diarmuid Ó'Murchú, *Quantum Theology: Spiritual Implications of the New Physics* (New York: Crossroad, 1997) 63–90. See also, however, the cautionary words of Tony Kelly in *An Expanding Theology*, 40–54.

38 Pannenberg, *Toward a Theology of Nature*, 33.

decisive as to how that scientific description is to be interpreted theologically and integrated into a coherent description of reality as a whole.[39] In the light of that event, it is possible to articulate a vision of creation that is grounded on love, in such a manner that it brings to the fore two inherent characteristics of materiality: relationality and openness to future fulfilment.

Creatio ex amore

In the Christian vision, the world in its entirety stands in a relationship to God as creature to Creator. The awesome depths of that relationship become fully manifest in Jesus Christ, in whom God becomes human and communicates with the world in a way that both defines it and perfects it. In this perspective, the world is not simply constituted by mindless matter, as some scientists would have us believe. On the contrary, as the arena of encounter between God and humanity, its transformation by the life, death and resurrection of Jesus Christ is one of the fruits of the encounter.[40]

In light of the foregoing, it is clear to the Christian that ultimate reality is finally personal and is defined by relationality and by love: God is love (1 Jn 4:8,16) – therein lies ultimate mystery and perfect simplicity – and Jesus Christ is nothing other than that love made visible in human form. He, then, establishes the benchmark for everything else that exists, and that includes the entire creation, brought into existence out of nothing, for no other motive than the gratuity of divine love. As Joseph Ratzinger reminds us, 'the universe is not the product of darkness and unreason. It comes from intelligence, freedom, and from the beauty that is identical with love'.[41] For that reason, some theologians today highlight that particular emphasis by suggesting that the traditional axiom, 'creation

---

39   See Nichols, *The Sacred Cosmos*, 215–217.
40   See von Balthasar, *The Glory of the Lord*, I, 303. See also McGrath, *A Scientific Theology*, I, 190–191; and McGrath, *A Scientific Theology*, II, 313.
41   Ratzinger, *In the Beginning*, 25.

out of nothing', needs to be supplemented with another, 'creation out of love'. Catherine LaCugna develops the point as follows: 'The reason for creation lies entirely in the unfathomable mystery of God, who is self-originating *and* self-communicating love. While the world is the gracious result of divine freedom, God's freedom means *necessarily* being who and what God is. From this standpoint the world is not created *ex nihilo* but *ex amore, ex condilectio*, that is, out of divine love'.[42]

Originating in God, who called it into being, and continually dependent on God, who never ceases to underpin it, creation finds its reason for existence in the infinite and eternal communion of Father, Son and Holy Spirit. It is precisely within this framework of trinitarian love that creation has to be situated simply as a gift of God, a gratuitous manifestation of trinitarian love. For, as von Balthasar explains, 'any world only has its place within that distinction between Father and Son that is maintained and bridged by the Holy Spirit... Everything temporal takes place within the embrace of the eternal action and as its consequence ...'.[43] Understood along these lines, creation is nothing other than a drama that plays out against a divine background: a drama of divine love in

---

42   Catherine Mowry LaCugna, *God for Us: The Trinity and Christian Life* (San Francisco: HarperCollins, 1991) 355. See also Elizabeth T. Groppe, 'Creation *ex nihilo* and *ex amore*: Ontological Freedom in the Theologies of John Zizioulas and Catherine Mowry LaCugna', *Modern Theology* 21/3 (July 2005) 463–496, at 471–472. Paul S. Fiddes develops a similar approach in 'Creation Out of Love', in John Polkinghorne (ed.), *The Work of Love: Creation as Kenosis* (Grand Rapids, Michigan: Eerdmans, London: SPCK, 2001) 167–191. The traditional insistence on 'creation out of nothing' is looked on suspiciously by some philosophers and theologians today, on the grounds that it reflects an overly metaphysical and patriarchal bias. See John D. Caputo, *The Weakness of God: A Theology of the Event* (Bloomington and Indianapolis: Indiana University Press, 2006); and Catherine Keller, *Face of the Deep: A Theology of Becoming* (London and New York: Routledge, 2003) esp. 43–64.

43   Hans Urs von Balthasar, *Theo-Drama: Theological Dramatic Theory*, Vol. IV, *The Action*, trans. Graham Harrison (San Francisco: Ignatius Press, 1994) 327. See also John J. O'Donnell, *The Mystery of the Triune God* (London: Sheed and Ward, 1988) 159–172; and Denis Edwards, *The God of Evolution: A Trinitarian Theology* (New York/Mahwah, N.J.: Paulist Press, 1999) 24–34.

which the universe is oriented towards union with God, therein to find completion and wholeness.[44] Thus, as Ratzinger remarks, 'communion with God is true reality, and by comparison with it everything, no matter how massively it asserts itself, is a phantom, a nothing.... [C]ommunication with God *is* reality. It is true reality, the really real, more real, even, than death itself'.[45]

Openness to Transcendence

At the heart of this theological approach is an understanding of universe in relational terms. The world and all that is in it are fundamentally characterised and defined by relationship: primarily the relationship with the transcendent Creator, which underpins a whole network of relationships among creatures themselves at every level of existence from the quantum to the cosmic.[46] Creation, then, is eminently reasonable and entirely relational, characteristics which are obviously manifest in the universe and which science has done much both to conceal and to uncover. It has concealed the relationality in a variety of ways already critiqued: for example, by the extremely narrow rationalistic outlook that it has adopted and that comes to expression in atomistic, mechanistic and reductionistic emphases, which seek to comprehend reality by breaking it up into its smallest constituent parts, as if that were sufficient to explain everything. Many scientists in recent years, however, have come to see that this approach is misguided, to say the least. In particular, the ecological approach to the sciences stresses the inter-relatedness of every organism and species in the world. For at each level of life and activity, organisms and species enter into relationships and patterns of cooperation to form wholes that

---

44   See Hans Urs von Balthasar, *Theo-Drama: Theological Dramatic Theory*, Vol. II, *Dramatis Personae: Man in God*, trans. Graham Harrison (San Francisco: Ignatius Press, 1990) 53.
45   Ratzinger, *Eschatology*, 89; see also 155.
46   See Jürgen Moltmann, *God and Creation: An Ecological Doctrine of Creation* (London: SCM Press, 1985) 11.

are greater than the sum of their parts, thereby bringing extraordinary richness and diversity to the world that would otherwise not exist.[47]

The Christian vision of life and of the world sees everything bound up in a 'web of relationships'[48] that ultimately originates in and finds its completion in the Triune God. It is in this trinitarian perspective too that the intelligibility actively pursued by scientists finds theological expression.[49] Far from viewing theology and science as implacable enemies, this stance holds that no genuine conflict exists between them, but that they can actually learn much from one another: theology learning from science in respect of the amazing processes that go on in the natural world in every sphere and at every level, thereby arriving at a deeper understanding of God's mysterious ways of interacting with creation; yet science too learning from theology in respect both of the ultimate underpinnings and finality of its entire project and how they fit into a coherent, transcendent whole.[50]

An approach that follows the holistic stance implied above will give considerable weight to the relational character of all life in the universe, to the unity-in-difference that informs it, and to the openness, interconnectedness and interdependence that characterises it at every level. To be, in this perspective, is to be in relationship.[51] To adapt the words of

47 See Denis Edwards, *Ecology at the Heart of Faith: The Change of Heart that Leads to a New Way of Living on Earth* (Maryknoll, New York: Orbis Books, 2006) 79–80; Bruteau, *God's Ecstasy*, 111; and McGrath, *A Scientific Theology*, II, 99.

48 The expression is used by Gerald O'Collins in *Jesus Risen: The Resurrection – What Actually Happened and What Does It Mean?* (London: Darton, Longman & Todd, 1987) 185. See also Bernard P. Prusak, 'Bodily Resurrection in Catholic Perspectives', *Theological Studies* 61/1 (March 2000) 64–105, at 81.

49 See John Polkinghorne, *Science and the Trinity: The Christian Encounter with Reality* (London: SPCK, 2004) esp. 60–87; and Polkinghorne, *Quantum Physics and Theology*, 99–104 and 110.

50 See Bruteau, *God's Ecstasy*, 44. The notion that God works in and through natural selection has been proposed, but Dawkins dismisses the whole notion vehemently as subterfuge and laziness on the part of God (see 118 [143–144]).

51 See Edwards, *Ecology at the Heart of Faith*, 78–81; also Bruteau, *God's Ecstasy*, 47; and Haught, *God after Darwin*, 161.

the poet John Donne, no creature of any sort – not even the tiniest and remotest and most fragmentary of particles – stands alone, an island entire of itself and defining of itself in the vast cosmos. For all exist in relationship not only to God, the transcendent cause who continues to underpin that existence, but in relation to the cosmos as a whole and to each other, however flimsy or tenuous any specific interaction or relationship might be. Those relationships are ultimately defining of every finite reality, in the openness and movement to transcendence they exhibit and in their capacity to be integrated into wholes greater than themselves: from subatomic particles to atomic ones; from atoms to molecules; from lifeless molecules to life-bearing ones; and up the chain of material evolution to human life and the realm of the spirit, at the apex of which is God, the initiator and sustainer of the entire process.[52]

Though clearly the vast majority of scientists are still far from accepting such a scheme, it is also evident that at least some of them are beginning to dissociate themselves from the wholly reductionist materialism that is still commonplace in the biological sciences. In physics, for example, particles are now conceived not as isolated material units but in terms of their interactions with other particles through the various fields and forces that are found in nature. A similar approach employed at the biological level would shift the focus from discrete biological entities to the processes and interrelationships between them that allow new and more complex forms of life, which transcend previous ones, to emerge.[53] Far from 'selfishness' being a defining characteristic of life at the genetic level, or indeed any other level of reality, this perspective would highlight the even more fundamental relationality that constitutes every entity with

---

52   For further references and reflections on the topic, see Haught, *Christianity and Science*, 91–95; and Judy Cannato, *Radical Amazement: Contemplative Lessons from Black Holes, Supernovas, and Other Wonders of the Universe* (Notre Dame, Indiana: Sorin Books, 2006) 84–86, 95–102.

53   For a discussion of the topic, see Nichols, *The Sacred Cosmos*, esp. 106–124. See also Mackey, *Christianity and Creation*, 362–363; Dyson, 'Our Biotech Future', 4; Polanyi, *Personal Knowledge*, esp. 381–405; and Pannenberg, *Toward a Theology of Nature*, 22–24.

respect to the rest of reality and ultimately to God. Thus, springing from the interactions that continually take place at every level of reality, new relationships arise to 'produce a richness that is not possessed by the components apart from these relationships'.[54]

Recognition that the findings of science give us invaluable insight into the world in no way precludes the activity of God, but actually serves to show how that activity is much more mysterious than we have hitherto imagined. Notwithstanding its appeal to many believers, it has to be acknowledged that the designer approach that Dawkins sets out to demolish in his work presents far too simplistic a model of the divine creativity in the world.[55] Apart from anything else, in the globalised world we inhabit, the 'designer' label is loaded with connotations that are far from Christian and that when pushed to the limit stand at odds with the traditional emphasis on creation as literally 'out of nothing'. Much more fundamentally, however, a rigid adherence to a designer approach to creation could easily result in a form of determinism that is every bit as distorting as the mechanistic equivalent already critiqued.[56] W. H. Vanstone argues the point insightfully, as he points out how popular devotion often misinterprets the God of enduring love 'as the God of foreordained and programmed purposes. It is assumed that for that to which He gives purpose He already has purpose, and that of that which He uses He has predetermined the use. To make this assumption is ... to reduce the divine activity to a kind of *production* – a mere drawing out, or display, of that which already is'.[57] Whatever credibility the designer model had in a highly structured and perfectly ordered world, where everything moves with clockwork regularity according to precisely determined natural laws that explain everything and leave nothing to chance, it has extremely little in a world where chaos, indeterminacy, randomness,

54 Edwards, *Ecology at the Heart of Faith*, 80.
55 See Haught, *God after Darwin*, 2–9.
56 See Pannenberg, *Toward a Theology of Nature*, 72–122, esp. 76–86.
57 W. H. Vanstone, *Love's Endeavour, Love's Expense: The Response of Being to the Love of God* (London: Darton, Longman & Todd, 1977) 65. See also Beattie, *The New Atheists*, 167–169.

probability and unceasing flux are writ large in the processes of nature
itself. In this new perspective, where inflexible notions of causality are
inadequate, a credible theological approach to the God-world relationship has to take these factors into account too.[58]
    In attempting to come to grips with these insights, theologians today
have not been slow to propose a variety of other models by which divine
agency might be conceived in light of the findings of contemporary science.[59] Notwithstanding the imperative to find and articulate such models
of God's action in the world, however, the traditional theological distinction between primary causality and secondary causality remains as
insightful and relevant as ever: the former clearly identifying God the
Creator as the primary, transcendent cause of all things, the latter refer-
ring to the various secondary agents which have been endowed by God
with the capacity for independent action in the created realm. As Neil
Ormerod expresses it in relation to human beings, they 'are true causes
of their own free acts, but only secondary causes, for God remains transcendent cause of all that is'.[60] In this perspective, all secondary agents are
sustained by and remain open to the divine power, which grounds and
underpins all reality, thereby allowing them to become vehicles of divine
action in God's ongoing providential care for the world. In the words of
Elizabeth Johnson, 'the mystery of the living God acts in and through
the creative acts of finite agents which have genuine causal efficacy in
their own right'.[61]

---

58   See Wolfhart Pannenberg, *Faith and Reality* (London: Search Press, Philadelphia:
      Westminster Press, 1977) 1–7; Davies, *The Creativity of God*, esp. 95–116; and Fiddes,
      'Creation Out of Love', 186–187.
59   See, for example, the brief overview by Elizabeth A. Johnson, *Quest for the Living
      God: Mapping Frontiers in the Theology of God* (New York and London: Continuum,
      2007) 191–197; and the more extended overview by Ward, *The Big Questions in
      Science and Religion*, 244–271.
60   Ormerod, 'Chance and Necessity, Providence and God', 269. In this essay, he presents
      a very spirited defence of the classical approach over against other approaches that
      seek to move beyond it. See also Jean Porter, *Nature as Reason: A Thomistic Theory
      of the Natural Law* (Grand Rapids, Michigan: Eerdmans, 2005) 82–103.
61   Johnson, *Quest for the Living God*, 193.

Openness to the Future

In responding to the challenges posed by scientific discoveries, theologians today highlight the openness to newness and possibility that is writ large in the universe itself, which as yet remains incomplete. For example, though highly complex and chaotic, the natural processes and interactions that take place at every level of reality are, at the same time, far from haphazard but are deeply patterned and intelligible too, displaying an intrinsic openness to new and beautiful combinations and always opening out to the future.[62]

The openness to newness and possibility, the actual creativity woven into the fabric of the universe itself, is perhaps nowhere rendered more explicit than in the phenomenon of human language in its various dimensions and in the speech acts which it enables us to make. Though hugely restricted because the number of phonemes (smallest units of sound) is quite limited, language itself opens out in an astonishing manner to form a vast array of words that can in turn be combined in extraordinarily creative ways to describe the world. For example, with reference just to the English language, Beatrice Bruteau makes the point that though the language contains a mere forty-four phonemes, that limited number can be combined in various ways to form the several million words characteristic of English; and, indeed, that this number of words is increasing by two hundred thousand each year. She continues:

> But the real astonishment comes when the words are arranged to form sentences. Sentences don't represent objects or actions; they represent propositions, assertions about how it is with the world, and reactions to the world and feelings about the world, and so on. How many sentences are there? We laugh. We know that's an absurd question. An endless number. There's no limit on the sentences we can

62   For a variety of approaches to this issue, see Haught, *Christianity and Science*, 95–96; Haught, *God after Darwin*, 165–184; Ormerod, *Creation, Grace, and Redemption*, 10–13 and 27–30; Ormerod, 'Chance and Necessity, Providence and God', 270–275; and John Polkinghorne, 'Kenotic Creation and Divine Action', in John Polkinghorne (ed.), *The Work of Love*, 90–106.

make out of our several million increasing by hundreds of thousands words made
out of forty-four phonemes. Finitude has been turned into infinitude.[63]

Though strictly bounded, just like the language we speak and the world of
which we are a part, the human spirit is open to newness and oriented to
infinitude, denying mortality, as it were, and thrusting forward dynamically towards future self-realisation and transcendent possibility. That
forward looking, transcendent orientation is reflected in the very structure
of human language itself, as George Steiner makes clear in reflecting on
the significance of the future tense and of the subjunctive: 'There is an
actual sense in which every human use of the future tense of the verb "to
be" is a negation, however limited, of mortality'.[64]

The negation of mortality is critically at variance with the stance
adopted by the advocates of evolutionary materialism, which, as we have
seen from *The God Delusion*, insists on the temporary nature of spirit and
the absolute finality of death. In the view of John Haught, the causal stance
that is explicit in that materialism amounts to nothing but a 'metaphysics
of the past', so rigidly fixated on what has already taken place that genuine
novelty is excluded and life today in all its diversity is viewed as simply
the unfolding of what is implicit in all that has gone before: 'nothing
more than an "algorithmic" process, fully explainable by tracing present
outcomes back to their determining physical causes in the past. All we
need to understand the present ... is to practice "reverse engineering."'[65]
In sharp contrast, Haught draws on the biblical data and the work of
other theologians to sketch a 'metaphysics of the future',[66] which views
God as the 'Absolute Future' who relates to the world not by compul-
sion but alluringly and 'in mode of promise', thereby summoning forth
its potentiality and calling forth new life as time continually opens out to

63   Bruteau, *God's Ecstasy*, 150. See also Steiner, *Grammars of Creation*, 130.
64   Steiner, *Grammars of Creation*, 5.
65   Haught, *God after Darwin*, 86. See also Haught, *Christianity and Science*,
     61–64.
66   Haught, *God after Darwin*, 83; and Haught, *Christianity and Science*, 7

the future.[67] In this faith perspective, 'it is the "future" that comes to meet us, takes hold of us, and makes us new'.[68] In other words, it is the creation's dynamic openness to a future full of surprising possibilities, not its grinding emergence out of a deterministic past, that underpins novelty in the universe and leads all its processes on the path of transformation.[69]

The orientation to the future for which Haught, and others too, argue integrates neatly with the eschatological thrust of Christian faith, which looks forward in hope to the new creation in Christ, his second coming and the consummation of all things in the glory of his resurrection. That eschatological orientation is ultimately defining of creation for the Christian.

67   See Haught, *God after Darwin*, 84–85. Haught also identifies and critiques a Platonic influence in Western theology and spirituality that views creation and the process of becoming in terms of a fall from timeless perfection: a 'metaphysics of the "eternal present," according to which the natural world is the always deficient reflection of, if not a perverse deviation from, a primordial perfection of "being" that exists forever ...' Haught, *God after Darwin*, 85. Jürgen Moltmann too argues along similar lines, suggesting a switch from 'the metaphysics of reality to a metaphysics of possibility ...' See Moltmann, 'God's Kenosis in the Creation and Consummation of the World', in John Polkinghorne (ed.), *The Work of Love*, 137–151, at 150.

68   Haught, *God after Darwin*, 89. See also Polkinghorne, *Science and the Trinity*, 78–82; and Caputo, *The Weakness of God*, 32–37.

69   It seems that physicists, because of new discoveries in quantum theory, are slowly beginning to grapple with possibilities along these lines. Davies suggests that quantum physics is now actually attempting to come to terms with 'retrocausality' or 'backward causation', in a manner that might be described as 'teleology without teleology'. Davies, *The Goldilocks Enigma*, 280. Considering an expanded version of the multiverse hypothesis that allows for all possible laws to be instantiated somewhere, he make the point that 'if universes with teleological laws exist, ours would be an excellent candidate. The universe certainly looks as if it possesses teleological features. Well, perhaps it is teleological!' Davies, *The Goldilocks Enigma*, 323–324, n.28. See also Patrick Barry, 'What's Done Is Done ...' *New Scientist* 191/2571 (30 September 2006) 36–39.

The Story and the Music of the Cosmos

As the handiwork of God, the divine Artist, creation is an event that can be explored at different levels, each of which has its own methodology or grammatical form. The dominant forms of exploration in the age in which we live are scientific and, through the scientific laws that have been elaborated, they have contributed enormously to our appreciation of the awesome beauty of the cosmos and to our understanding of its extraordinary complexity. But other forms of exploration are possible too: for example, through symbolic forms such as narrative and drama, art and music that, though very different grammatically from the sciences, are no less insightful in furnishing a multitude of avenues for exploring the divine creativity in terms of its human equivalent.[70]

As we have already seen, the Bible gives a privileged place to the narrative approach to creation. This approach remains important, because it never ceases to remind us that creation is an ongoing story – 'a narrative still in process'[71] and 'an open-ended adventure'[72] – that will be complete only when the divine Author brings everything to a conclusion at the end of time. As it now stands, therefore, creation is not yet the finished article; it is not yet perfected and not yet completely open to union with its Creator and Saviour. For that reason, the story of creation is not God's alone to tell; though God upholds the cosmos and all the processes taking place within it, the exercise of divine power is such that it does not predetermine everything that is to happen, but rather it allows cosmic interactions and processes the space and time in which to unfold in all their contingency, according to the appropriate natural laws. Thus, as time moves on and every created reality makes its own creative contribution to the ongoing narrative of the cosmos, all contributions are received graciously by God and, purified of imperfection, incorporated into the divine story that

70   On God as the 'Ultimate Artist' and creation as 'a work of art', see Mackey, *Christianity and Creation*, 49; and Vanstone, *Love's Endeavour, Love's Expense*, 39–74. On how Dawkins and other contemporary atheists reject explanations other than the scientific one, see Haught, *God and the New Atheism*, 84–91.

71   Haught, *Christianity and Science*, 45; see also 162–163.

72   Johnson, *Quest for the Living God*, 190.

began at the moment of creation and that will find its completion in the embrace of the Triune God at the moment of resurrection.[73]

Music is no less insightful a metaphor of creation. Indeed, it has been described as 'a pulse of creation',[74] while human history in its entirety has been compared to a symphony, to which all human beings contribute as their lives unfold. In the last analysis, however, it is the trinitarian God who, as composer and conductor, shapes the piece into a coherent whole, improvising and adjusting the music continually so that even the discordant notes and laboured playing of the human instrumentalists are beautifully transformed by the skills and ingenuity of the divine maestro.[75] Thus, to adapt the image slightly along lines suggested by Pierre Teilhard de Chardin, the 'hymn of the universe'[76] in praise of God finds its ultimate coherence, together with its perfect expression and fulfilment, in the glory of the risen Christ.

The more we look towards the future in hope as we await the glorious coming of Christ, however, the more problematic and jarring the discordance between what we aspire 'to play and sing' and what we actually do becomes. Hatred and division, violence and discord, are facts of everyday life and, as Dawkins's critique of religion forcefully reminds us, religious believers have contributed in no small measure to the evil that is characteristic of the human situation. The critical question thus emerges as to how Christian faith deals with this issue. Dawkins's approach may be inadequate on several counts, but is the theological approach any more coherent and credible?

73   See Haught, *Christianity and Science*, 162–163; and Beattie, *The New Atheists*, 167–169.
74   Ó'Murchú, *Quantum Theology*, 47.
75   See Herbert Butterfield, *Christianity and History* (London and Glasgow: Collins Fontana Books, 1957 [1949]) 124–125; also Aylward Shorter, *Revelation and Its Interpretation* (London: Geoffrey Chapman, 1983) 69, 100–101; Elizabeth Johnson, 'Does God Play Dice? Divine Providence and Chance', *Theological Studies* 57/1 (March 1996) 3–18, at 18; Arthur Peacocke, *Creation and the World of Science: The Re-Shaping of Belief* (Oxford: Oxford University Press, 2004) 104–111; Davies, *The Creativity of God*, 21–24, 167–168; and Caputo, *The Weakness of God*, 156.
76   Pierre Teilhard de Chardin, *The Hymn of the Universe* (London: Collins, 1965).

CHAPTER 5

Creation as Risk: The Foolishness of Divine Love

Theists believe that God tolerates evil to preserve human freedom. God set a limit on his omnipotence in order to give humans intelligence and the freedom to use it well or badly.... The obsequiousness of robots is not enough.
— WILLIAM J. O'MALLEY[1]

Does the scientific mode of expression suffice? Is that language, forbidding and superseding all other language, not also a sort of idolatry? Since the beginning of the new century, ... an old sentence of Martin Luther has been on my mind. 'Reason is a whore'; that is, it sleeps with everyone who pays. One look at gene technology is enough to confirm Luther's point.
— DOROTHEE SOELLE[2]

The irony of The God Delusion, *then, is that its author is the high priest of a new religion.*
— NICHOLAS LASH[3]

The work of Dawkins on the 'God hypothesis' challenges believers and unbelievers alike in relation to the ultimate stance they adopt towards life. In terms of the arguments from probability that he develops in support of his rejection of God, life ultimately amounts to a colossal gamble. The atheistic gambler's stance is straightforwardly rational and scientific and

1   O'Malley, *God: The Oldest Question*, 34.
2   Dorothee Soelle, *The Mystery of Death*, trans. Nancy Lukens-Rumscheidt and Martin Lukens-Rumscheidt (Minneapolis, MN: Fortress Press, 2007) 44.
3   Lash, 'Where Does *The God Delusion* Come from?', 521; and Lash, *Theology for Pilgrims*, 18.

it is oriented to lessening the risk of losing: to wager on the God hypothesis is utter folly, given the impossible odds against it and the total lack of scientific evidence in its favour; to wager on the gigantic 'luck' that kicks evolution into motion is perfectly reasonable, given our presence here and the scientific rationality that can explain it. By these standards, the Christian believer is most definitely a loser.

The paradox of Christian belief is such, however, that the aforementioned gamble is anything but straightforward. Granted that the universe and all that is in it appear to involve simply 'a gigantic roll of the dice',[4] as Einstein implied, the foolishness of belief is underpinned by the mysteriousness of divine love, manifest in the most paradoxical but complete way in Jesus Christ, the great 'loser' to judge by purely worldly standards. Far from being a lottery subject merely to the vagaries of chance, Jesus Christ reveals that what underpins and envelops the created order in its entirety – embracing not merely the 'gaps' in scientific explanations but also the random mutations, the particular interactions and contingent processes that have played and continue to play their own roles in enabling human life to assume its particular shape – is nothing other than the mystery of divine love. As Joseph Ratzinger, now Pope Benedict XVI, reminds us, 'only when we know that there is Someone who did not make a blind throw of the dice and that we have not come from chance but from freedom and love can we then, in our unnecessary-ness, be grateful for this freedom and know with gratitude that it is really a gift to be a human being'.[5]

To be human is to be fundamentally a gift, for each and every human being bears in a unique manner the imprint of the God who created them in freedom and love. Nowhere is the character of that gift more apparent than in our own human capacity for freedom and love, not simply in terms of our earthly relationships but also in our openness to perfect fulfilment in union with the God whose likeness we bear. Such fulfilment has been made possible for us by Jesus Christ.

4   Caputo, *The Weakness of God*, 128.
5   Ratzinger, *In the Beginning*, 53–54.

1. God's Wager on Human Freedom

For Christians, the life, death and resurrection of Jesus Christ constitute the fulcrum around which human life, the cosmos and history in their entirety turn. The revolution in understanding that he effected furnishes us with an absolute reference point in history, capable of being investigated by reason yet ultimately standing in indictment of all worldly standards, including both human reason and love. The mystery of Jesus Christ, in other words, constitutes the unsurpassable revelation of divine love that enables his followers come to a deeper understanding not only of God but of the entire created order, including human life and freedom.

Under the Sign of the Cross

At the level of the natural order of things, first of all, it is clear that life in this world is characterised by pain, suffering and waste, which often scandalise people and lead them to question the existence of God, most especially when catastrophic events such as earthquakes and tsunamis cause huge devastation and claim the lives of the innocent. The cry is often heard in such instances, why does God allow such suffering to occur and why does God not intervene to prevent such devastation and loss of life?

Though Christian faith proffers no easy answers to such questions, it does bring to the fore several levels of response. First of all, it points to the general laws which God set in place in bringing this world into existence. Those laws give expression to the coherence and regularities of nature and they allow natural events to unfold in a contingent manner, which is not determined and which involves a certain measure of independence from God, who remains their transcendent cause.[6] Such independence from

---

6   See Lonergan, *Insight*, 664. For an overview of the theological issues in question here, see Ormerod, 'Chance and Necessity, Providence and God', 263–278. See

God means, for example, that for an animal falling from a precipice, the 'law of gravity' runs its course, with inevitably fatal consequences in this instance. Likewise, in the case of natural disasters involving the loss of life, the outcome is largely dependent on the natural circumstances prevailing and the scientific laws, both classical and statistical, to which they are subject. In a universe where natural events are contingent and not necessary and where God does not routinely intervene to dictate the outcome of those events, accidents are inevitable and suffering is unavoidable.[7]

The suffering that is found in nature notwithstanding, secondly, the light generated by the cross and resurrection of Jesus Christ enables Christians to see with St Paul that the 'groaning' of creation and the travails of every living creature during its limited time here on earth are not wasted (see Rom 8:18–22). As it awaits redemption in Jesus Christ, nature itself in all its contingency stands under the sign of the cross, the very sign *of the Lamb that was slaughtered from the foundation of the world'* (Rev 13:8).[8] The cruciform shape it thus displays constitutes an enduring reminder of its limitations and vulnerability to decay, on the one hand, and an enduring offer of hope and life, on the other.[9] In Christ crucified and risen, then, suffering, decay and death are not the end of the story; they are but gateways to life without end.

At the level of human life and freedom, thirdly, the cross sheds light on the evil and suffering that plagues the human condition, as it lays bare the dynamics of how human beings relate to God, to one another and to the world. To be more specific, the death of Jesus, the wholly innocent human being who is God Incarnate, exposes just how clearly amiss are

---

also Johnson, 'Does God Play Dice? Divine Providence and Chance', 3–18; and Pannenberg, *Toward a Theology of Nature*, 34–37.

7   See Haught, *Christianity and Science*, 94; also Keith Ward, *Pascal's Fire: Scientific Faith and Religious Understanding* (Oxford: Oneworld, 2006) 66.

8   This is the alternative translation furnished in a footnote by the NRSV. See also Arthur Peacocke, 'The Cost of New Life', in John Polkinghorne (ed.), *The Work of Love*, 21–42, at 41.

9   See the reflections on 'cruciform nature' by Holmes Rolston, III, in 'Kenosis and Nature', in John Polkinghorne (ed.), *The Work of Love*, 43–65, at 58–61.

things in this world: how human creativity so easily goes awry and can be used to destroy the earth rather than enhance it; and how relationality simply becomes a power game in which only the strongest and the fittest survive. In bringing to the fore too the foolishness of divine wisdom and the weakness of divine strength (see 1 Cor 1:24–31), his death exposes the shallow posturing of human reason's claims to absolute authority in every sphere and the dangerous consequences that follow in the wake of such claims. And, yet, the cross is the sign of hope for human beings in their weakness and arrogance too, as the life and death of Jesus made abundantly clear to his disciples.

The Revelation of Divine Vulnerability

Though the followers of Jesus dispersed in the immediate aftermath of his death, his resurrection from the dead had an extraordinary impact on that group of weak and frightened people, empowering them to re-group, filling them with insight into what Jesus was really about and transforming them into powerful witnesses of his Gospel. At the basic level of their own understanding of Jesus, their encounter with him risen from the dead enabled them to see that he was utterly unique in every way: the messenger of the kingdom of God whose death revealed him to be its fulfilment; the Messiah, who is our redemption in person (1 Cor 1:18); the Son of God, the eternal beloved of the Father, who has become incarnate in our midst to take away the sins of the world (see Mk 15:39; 9:2–8; and Jn 1:29). That recognition too revolutionised the disciples' understanding of God, enabling them to see just how easily that understanding was distorted by human sin and violence. Far from being a God of vengeance who relishes violence and takes delight in inflicting punishments on all and sundry, God is entirely Light, without a trace of darkness or vindictiveness (1 Jn 1:5); and God is entirely Love, self-giving and self-emptying, whole, entire and perfect (1 Jn 1:8–16).

Their recognition of the divine identity of Jesus and his utter sinlessness turned the world of his disciples on its head, alerting them to the enormity of the sin that had led to his crucifixion. They came to see that the cross symbolised our human rejection of God and of God's ways of doing things in the world; they came to see too how deeply entrenched in violence and hatred is the world in which we live, a crucifying place that ruthlessly preys on weakness and innocence, even when undertaken as a commitment to 'law and order' and in the name of God (see Jn 11:49–52).[10] Those insights enabled them to recognise how the human mind is prone to self-deception (see 1 Cor 3:18–20), how the human heart is so open to seduction by pseudo-loves and to spurning genuine love when it is freely given, and how the human will inevitably makes the wrong choices, even when the desire to do the good is there (see Rom 7:21–23).

Yet that recognition of the enormous power, the depth and the capacity for evil of human beings was made possible by experience of divine forgiveness and mercy that preceded it in the encounter with the risen Christ; for, as St Paul so eloquently expressed it, 'where sin increased, grace abounded all the more' (Rom 5:20). Paradoxically, then, the resurrection of Christ from the dead reveals that it is where sin and evil are at their most destructive that God's grace is most powerfully active and God's love ultimately triumphant; it is precisely where our human capacity for evil achieves its zenith by killing the sinless Son of God that it is totally exposed to God's love and is resoundingly overcome. To put the matter briefly, redemption happens when our human worst is exposed to God's overwhelming love and is overcome by it (see Rom 5:6–8). Hence, if the cross of Christ symbolises our human sinfulness, even more so does it symbolise the extraordinary love of God in the act of overcoming that sinfulness.

For Christians, the mystery of the death and resurrection of Christ constitutes an extraordinary revelation of divine love in the act of overcoming the human sinfulness that lies at the root of evil in our world. The relevance of this for our critique needs to be further elaborated by drawing out its implications in a number of areas, beginning with the sinfulness of human beings and how that sinfulness distorts fundamentally

10   See Herbert McCabe, *Law, Love and Language* (London and New York: Continuum, 2003 [1968]) 132; also Joe Egan, *Brave Heart of Jesus: Mel Gibson's Postmodern Way of the Cross* (Dublin: The Columba Press, 2004).

our understanding of God. In this christological perspective, conventional human wisdom is subverted and turned entirely on its head by the foolishness of God (see 1 Cor 1:17–31). Likewise, the conventional perception of risk is shattered, for the death and resurrection of Christ reveal God to be utterly reckless in wagering everything on human freedom, in surrendering the success or failure of the entire project of creation into human hands, and to be utterly vulnerable in having to pay the price of that wager.

The Restlessness of the Human Heart

For Christian faith, God's totally gratuitous and loving act of creating human beings in the divine image and likeness (see Gen 1:27) renders them uniquely creative in their own right. In the final analysis, that creativity is finally identical with the extraordinary spiritual capacity for freedom that defines our humanity. Creation, as George Steiner observes, is practically synonymous with freedom: '*that which is enacted freedom and which includes and expresses in its incarnation the presence of what is absent from it or of what could be radically other*.'[11] Giving central stage to human freedom in this manner highlights clearly that the world is not a deterministic place, as some would have it. On the contrary, having been endowed with freedom, human beings have a uniquely creative role to play as collaborators with God in shaping the world in order to bring both it and themselves to fulfilment.

Viewing creation in terms of human freedom also brings clearly to the fore that God's creative act redounds on divine freedom itself to the extent that it establishes boundaries and limits for the exercise of divine power. In other words, the act of creation constitutes an extraordinary act of divine self-limitation in which God not only makes room for finite creaturely freedom but does so in a way that actually allows it to set itself

11 Steiner, *Grammars of Creation*, 108.

over against the infinite divine freedom.[12] Understood along these lines, the divine act of creation is finally nothing other than a wager on human freedom; a wager that is no less risky on God's part than is the wager on transcendence on the part of human beings. God, in creating the world as the arena for the exercise of human creativity in freedom, takes extraordinary risks: the risk that divine love will be spurned and rejected, the risk that human freedom will be abused and ultimately destroyed by its own wilful folly.[13] John Caputo spells it out clearly: 'For the creation is nothing if it is not a dicey business, both for God and for us. Life, existence, creation are nothing if not a risk; but for anyone worth their salt, they are what Levinas would call a "beautiful risk."'[14] To appreciate the beauty and enormity of that risk from a Christian standpoint, it is necessary to investigate more closely the dynamics of human freedom.

Shaped by love and made for it, oriented to it and desirous of it, the quest for understanding, meaning and truth – of which the scientific enterprise itself is a good illustration – is intrinsic to human identity. The identity of the human self is not simply given, already finalised and complete upon entering the world at the moment of birth. On the contrary, the self is endowed with an extraordinary spiritual power that renders it capable of determining its own identity and constituting itself in freedom over the course of a lifetime. Even with respect to those things that cannot be changed, that condition the self and that determine key aspects of its life – including genetic make-up, 'memetic' make-up if such a thing were ever shown to exist, and even death itself – the self is still free to the extent that it can choose the particular stance it adopts towards them. In that spiritual realm of freedom, wherein lies the key to human greatness, the openness of creation to God becomes explicit.

Endowed with such an extraordinary capacity, it is little wonder that the human spirit is ever restless: hungering, searching, exploring,

---

12   See von Balthasar, *Theo-Drama*, IV, 328–329; see also von Balthasar, *Theo-Drama*, II, 272–273.
13   See Fiddes, 'Creation out of Love', 184–191.
14   Caputo, *The Weakness of God*, 64; see also 176. See too Peacocke, 'The Cost of New Life', esp. 39–41.

questioning and wondering, in its relationship to the whole of reality and in its outreach to it. That restlessness, its desire for meaning and truth and love, is finally unbounded, without limits on this side of creation. 'Simply as desire', Neil Ormerod observes, 'it knows no limits'.[15] St Augustine's memorable address to God brings to the fore with insight the theological basis of this unlimited desire in the restlessness of the human heart for God: '... you have made us for yourself and our heart is restless until it rests in you.'[16] The human being, then, is fundamentally a seeker of relationships, a searcher for love that brings fulfilment, a questioner who never ceases to ask questions or to strive for deeper understanding, an explorer whose stance towards life opens out to the vast horizons of the cosmos, and even beyond; a communicator whose use of the future tense in language negates, in however limited a way, mortality itself. George Steiner reminds us powerfully of this when he argues that 'every use of an "if"-sentence tells of a refusal of the brute inevitability, of the despotism of the fact. "Shall", "will" and "if", circling in intricate fields of semantic force around a hidden centre or nucleus of potentiality, are the passwords to hope'.[17]

Far from being merely a licence to choose and do whatever one likes, as some appear to understand freedom, the anthropology briefly outlined above views it as a spiritual power constitutive of human existence itself, nothing less than the echo of the divine call within us inviting us to complete fulfilment. That extraordinary gift is capable of being perfected through the choices we make for wholesome and just relationships with others, amid the myriad choices and circumstances that make up our lives, and culminating finally in union with God. Yet the human choice for such relationships and such union is not compelled, for their opposite – turning one's back on others and on God – can equally be chosen, and chosen freely at that. The human heart may be restless for union with God, yet that restlessness offers no straightforward and assured guarantees that its goal will be attained. Human self-transcendence is, in actuality, quite

15   Ormerod, *Creation, Grace, and Redemption*, 32.
16   St Augustine, *Confessions*, Book I.i (1), 3.
17   Steiner, *Grammars of Creation*, 5; see also 13.

fraught and insecure, for freedom confers responsibility that we fear and
are reluctant to exercise;[18] a gift so precious and yet so precarious that
the cumulative effect of the decisions that human beings themselves have
taken since the dawn of consciousness has been to subvert the whole thrust
towards transcendence, to drag themselves and their descendants down
to a level lower than what is appropriately human, with a corresponding
diminishment of their capacity for freedom. A brief look at the Scriptures
and the Tradition of the Church indicates this very clearly.[19]

The Vulnerability of Freedom

In describing in symbolic terms the origins of human sinfulness, the
opening chapters of the book of Genesis indicate how human beings in
disobedience spurned this limited, earthbound existence in the illusory
conviction that an existence without limits was within their own grasp,
achievable by their own endeavours alone. In so doing, they violated the
divine prohibition that marked their existence and transgressed the limits
to which they were bound, thereby distorting first their relationship with
God and then with every living creature. Once those relationships were
thrown out of kilter, the knock-on effects rippled through every facet of
human existence, leading quickly to a situation where evil and sin came
to exercise a highly distorting influence throughout the entire world
and where the failure to achieve human fulfilment leads inevitably to
destructiveness.[20]

Reflecting on the topic of evil in the world in New Testament times,
in the light of the mystery of Jesus Christ, St Paul draws on the Genesis

18   Erich Fromm explores this topic from a psychological point of view in *The Fear of
      Freedom* (London: Routledge and Kegan Paul Ltd, 1960 [1942]).
19   See Lonergan, *Method in Theology*, 110–111.
20   See Lonergan, *Method in Theology*, 105. For an analysis of some key texts, see Paul
      Ricoeur, *The Symbolism of Evil*, trans. Emerson Buchanan (Boston: The Beacon
      Press, 1969) esp. 159–362. See also Tatha Wiley, *Original Sin: Origins, Developments,
      Contemporary Meanings* (New York/Mahwah, N.J.: Paulist Press, 2002) 29.

story to spell out how human beings, apart from Christ, live 'under the power of sin' (Rom 3:9), a contagion afflicting everybody, which can be traced back to the sin of Adam (Rom 5:12–21). Sin afflicts humanity so fundamentally that the law itself becomes an instrument of sin and the human will is disempowered in its efforts to do what is good.

> So I find it to be a law that when I want to do what is good, evil lies close at hand. For I delight in the law of God in my inmost self, but I see in my members another law at war with the law of my mind, making me captive to the law of sin that dwells in my members (Rom 7:21–23).

In thus arguing, Paul highlights a dimension of the human that the modern world in general and many of our contemporaries in particular, Dawkins included, completely ignore: the ultimate powerlessness of the will, even when knowledge of the good has been attained and the desire to do it is there.

The insights of Paul were later given more systematic expression in the writings of St Augustine and in the teaching of the Church on original sin. Of critical importance with regard to this teaching is Augustine's insight that evil is not a substance or reality in itself but a privation or lack; it is not a nature in itself but a choice or act of the will on the part of human beings.[21] The doctrine affirms too that sin is humanity's true situation before God, distorting each and every human self in a most fundamental way, even prior to the conscious choices of individuals and their sinful actions. The blame for this affliction can be laid squarely on human beings themselves, and its root cause can be traced to the sinful choices made by our earliest ancestors. The first or originating sin at the dawn of human history had a catastrophic impact on all that followed, setting in motion a spiralling process of sinfulness that impacts on everyone from their origin by depriving them of the grace of union with God. Hence, when the time for personal action comes, each and every person

---

21   See, for example, Stephen J. Duffy, 'Our Hearts of Darkness: Original Sin Revisited', *Theological Studies* 49/4 (October 1988) 597–622, at 601.

in turn re-enacts the break with God and thereby personally contributes to the sinfulness of the human condition.

Even though scientific discoveries in more recent times have shown that many of the cosmological and biological presuppositions Augustine held were seriously flawed, the relevance of his thought endures, for it tallies in numerous respects with what contemporary thought has brought to the fore about the human condition. In thus considering the issue of original sin nowadays, theologians are able to draw on the insights of other disciplines – for example, psychology, the social sciences and biology – to reinterpret aspects of the doctrine, most especially as it bears on the drama of human freedom.[22] In focusing the light of faith on that issue, the doctrine of original sin highlights how that fundamental capacity for self-determination has been undermined from the very beginning by a self-centredness that subverts the whole thrust towards a genuine self-transcending outreach to God and to others. The relationships thus arising, not only among human beings themselves but also with God and with every living creature, are inevitably distorted, and they contribute to an ongoing spiral of human sinfulness that leaves no sphere of life untarnished. In other words, due to the cumulative effect of sinful choices going back to the dawn of human consciousness and action, the human self finds itself incapable of exercising the self-transcending freedom that constitutes it without violating its relationships with God and with others at every level of existence: personal, social, cultural and systemic.[23] The problem of evil is thus fundamentally a human problem, the outcome of sinful choices by human beings who have acted and continue to act in such ways that their power to do good is seriously impaired. The moral evil that is so clearly evident in the world comes neither from God nor from nature, but from human freedom.

The relevance of the above reflections for our critique of Dawkins's work comes to the fore at this point. As we have previously seen, his case against the 'God hypothesis' hinges on his appeal to probability to show

22   See the various essays in *Original Sin: A Code of Fallibility*, ed. Christophe Boureux and Christoph Theobald, *Concilium* (2004/1).
23   On sin as a rejection of relationality, see Ratzinger, *In the Beginning*, 73.

that God does not exist. Strange as it may seem, Christian faith does not preclude the use of statistical probability entirely in religious matters, but the above reflections on original sin most certainly imply that its correct use applies not to transcendent divine realm, but rather to us in our earthbound, matter of fact, historical and sinful condition. More specifically, as Neil Ormerod reminds us while following the approach charted by Bernard Lonergan, it applies to the reality of original sin, which is 'a statistical, not a classical law. It is a statistical law, with probability one ...'[24] Original sin, in other words, is not a necessary or ontological constituent of human beings; it is rather a contingent, historical reality that arises from the misuse of human freedom through wrong choices and evil actions. Such has been the detrimental impact of those choices and actions on human life and society over the course of history, moreover, that freedom itself as it now stands is fundamentally compromised, to such an extent that further sin is inevitable when we come to act. David Tracy summarises the discussion: 'That inevitability allows one to understand how each human being, first trapped in a social situation where evil is clearly present, then unable to continue the constant reflection needed to ward off the habitual inclination to evil ("original sin"), eventually cannot but sin (*non posse non peccare*), yet does so freely and responsibly.'[25] In the Christian view of life, human beings are indeed free, but so fragile is that freedom and so vulnerable to distortion that its exercise inevitably compounds the legacy of human evil that characterises human life and society at every level.

The endemic sinfulness of human beings that renders human freedom incredibly fragile has knock-on effects in every sphere of life.[26] Human history gives testimony to those effects in its accounts of the wars, the deaths, the pillaging and the barbaric acts that characterise every era, not

24   Ormerod, *Creation, Grace, and Redemption*, 81. See also Bernard Lonergan, *Grace and Freedom: Operative Grace in the Thought of St. Thomas Aquinas*, ed. J. Patout Burns (New York: Herder and Herder, 1971) 46–53.
25   David Tracy, *Blessed Rage for Order: The New Pluralism in Theology* (Minneapolis, MN: The Winston – Seabury Press, 1975) 212.
26   See Pope Benedict XVI, *Spe Salvi*, esp. par. 24 and 30.

148   CHAPTER 5

least our own. And, as the Genesis accounts of creation suggest, even
nature itself is not exempt from the effects of human sinfulness – a fact
to which current fears about climate change bear abundant witness. All
of this highlights in quite dramatic fashion the vulnerability of God's
creation itself.

11. The Vulnerability of Creation

In dealing above with the reality of sin in the world, the restlessness of
the human heart has been highlighted to draw attention to the spiritual
nature of human freedom as unbounded and as ultimately oriented to
God. The issue of how that restlessness is interpreted and understood is
absolutely critical for our study, because Dawkins, in the course of *The
God Delusion*, adverts to the same issue, all the while denying the spiritual
any basis in reality other than the material.

Reflecting in *The God Delusion* on the possibility of a 'god centre'
(169 [197]) or 'God-shaped gap' (347 [388]), Dawkins indicates that
Darwinian scientists like himself will still want to understand the natural selection processes that favoured it. He then asks a profound question: 'But could it be that God clutters up a gap that we'd be better off
filling with something else? Science, perhaps? Art? Human friendship?
Humanism? Love of this life in the real world ...' (347 [388]).[27] In framing the question in this manner and outlining some indicative answers to
it, Dawkins alerts us to a destructive folly long since exposed in biblical
revelation: namely, idolatry. For the Christian believer, the 'God-shaped
gap' is all too apparent in the openness of the human heart to God and in
its restless longing; likewise, however, attempting to plug that gap and to

27   Though the image of the 'gap' is a valid one, it is not without flaws, for, as Denys
     Turner reminds us, 'creatures are more distinct from each other than God can
     possibly be from any of them. The logic of transcendence is not best embodied in
     metaphors of "gaps" ...' *Faith Seeking* (London: SCM Press, 2002) 18.

fill its emptiness with merely created things, rather than entering into a relationship with the God who ultimately brought it into existence and who alone can complete it, itself amounts to nothing other than highly delusory and utterly destructive folly.

Human Grasping

As the biblical witness makes clear, the entry of sin into the world fundamentally compromised human freedom and led to distortions in human relationships at every level, not least in the relationship with God. In the symbolic terms of the creation story from the book of Genesis, for example, it is clear that human disobedience seriously distorted and undermined the human capacity for relationship, not least with God, with grave consequences for human existence. Having violated the divine prohibition and transgressed the limit to which they were bound, the human couple are expelled from the Garden, condemned to live a finite existence outside paradise, separately from and no longer in close relationship to their Creator. The effects of this alienation gradually become evident, with relationships deteriorating across the board and leading humans to delude themselves to the extent that they think they can transgress every limit, even to the extent of reaching heaven by their own powers. The story of the attempt to construct the tower of Babel (Gen 11:1–9) shows the depths of the folly to which they can sink.

The relevance of that story from Genesis, and of other biblical stories too, endures, for at every level the world is still characterised by distorted, sinful relationships that tend towards breakdown and even violence. Hence, the social conditioning and all the other types of conditioning that characterise humanity, beginning even in the womb, leave no one immune and unaffected. Even from birth, the negative effects of that conditioning become apparent, as the ego turns inward and the heart becomes enchained, so that self-centredness inevitably becomes the underlying dynamic in its every relationship. As that me-centredness is confirmed and strengthened by the various choices the self eventually comes to make – and here perhaps Dawkins's reflections on the 'me-me'

could conceivably contribute some useful insights, though obviously
not in the manner he intends – all the facets and parameters of its life
are impaired, including the capacity of reason to know what is good and
the capacity of the will to do it. Thus, self-delusion flourishes and selfish
grasping comes to characterise human action, with detrimental consequences for every human relationship, including the relationship with
God.[28] As in the other areas outlined above, here again St Augustine has
much to teach us.

It was the insight of Augustine that no created good can satisfy the
restlessness of the human heart, which finds perfect fulfilment in God
alone. Unable to enter lovingly into a fulfilling relationship with God
because of sin, however, the heart, intent on satiating its desires, grasps at
straws and seeks to cling to them, thereby succeeding merely in whetting
further its desires and exacerbating its own unhappiness and insecurity.
The disparity between the boundlessness of human desire and the capacity of what desire can actually achieve by its own power merely leads
to the frustration and emptiness that finally tears human society apart.
Imperial Rome, for Augustine, offers a perfect illustration of the dynamic
of the 'earthly city' at work here: desirous of 'an earthly peace' while still
'the slave of base passions', it condemns itself to 'the mad pursuit of war'
in order to acquire the earthly goods that ostensibly promise to deliver
peace to their possessor. The inevitable consequence of cherishing and
pursuing those ephemeral goods, to the neglect of the 'higher goods' that
belong to the 'city on high', however, 'is fresh misery, and an increase of
the wretchedness already there'.[29]

28   For a further exploration of these ideas, see James Alison, *The Joy of Being Wrong:
      Original Sin through Easter Eyes* (New York: Crossroad, 1998).
29   St Augustine, *City of God*, trans. Henry Bettenson (London: Penguin Books, 2003
      [1972]), Book XIV, chapter 4, page 600 – henceforth cited in the form 14.4, 600
      – and 3.10, 97. See the comments of Thomas W. Smith, 'The Glory and Tragedy
      of Politics', in John Doody, Kevin L. Hughes, and Kim Paffenroth (eds), *Augustine
      and Politics* (Lanham, Maryland: Lexington Books, 2005) 187–213, at 198–199.

According to Augustine, the same dynamic is manifest in the pro-
liferation of Roman gods[30] and the 'ludicrous nonsense'[31] about them,
to which even the wisest Romans adhere in assigning 'particular gods
to particular spheres and to almost every single movement',[32] including
responsibility for the preservation and extension of the empire itself.[33] For
example, convinced that happiness is the remit of the gods and yet in a
quandary because they did not know the name of the giver of happiness,
the people of Rome 'decided to call him by the name of the gift for which
they believed him responsible ... the name "Felicity."'[34] Yet 'the inclusion
of Felicity in the ranks of the gods' was itself quite infelicitous, in that it
was followed by the devastation of civil war.[35] Boasting of the grandeur
of the empire in such circumstances – where life is lived 'amid the hor-
rors of war' and the shedding of human blood, 'under the shadow of fear
and amid the terror of ruthless ambition' – is anything but reasonable
or sensible; for 'the only joy to be attainted had the fragile brilliance of
glass, a joy outweighed by the fear that it may be shattered in a moment'.[36]
Augustine's conclusion is devastating:

> These fools turn the gifts of God into deities, and by the obstinacy of their insolent
> self-will, offend the God who confers those gifts. How can a man escape unhappi-
> ness, if he worships Felicity as divine and deserts God, the giver of felicity? Could
> a man escape starvation by licking the painted picture of a loaf, instead of begging
> real bread from someone who had it to give?[37]

In brief, by attempting 'to ensure the insignificant and deceptive happiness of this world',[38] through the worship of idols that were simply the

---

30 See St Augustine, *City of God*, 3.12, 100–101.
31 St Augustine, *City of God*, 4.31, 176.
32 St Augustine, *City of God*, 4.16, 155.
33 St Augustine, *City of God*, 4.8, 143.
34 St Augustine, *City of God*, 4.25, 166.
35 See St Augustine, *City of God*, 4.23, 163.
36 St Augustine, *City of God*, 4.3, 138.
37 St Augustine, *City of God*, 4.23, 165.
38 St Augustine, *City of God*, 3.17, 112; see also 3.18, 117.

deluded manifestations of its own longing instead of through worship of the living God, Rome brought on itself untold trouble that merely condemned it to perpetual unhappiness and misery.[39]

The inextricable links between human sinfulness and delusory religious beliefs that Augustine identifies operating in Roman society are far from being the exclusive preserve of that ancient society. On the contrary, they are as old as society itself and, notwithstanding the enormous strides that have been taken in practically every sphere of life, they remain operative in every time and place, including our own.

Idols of Destruction

The breakdown in the relationship with God brought about by sinful human actions and choices leads inevitably to distortions in the concept of God that people hold. The Bible documents that struggle in the life and history of Israel, and it pulls no punches in showing how even the high and mighty fell into that trap, with all its destructive fallout.

In the biblical view of things, human creatures alone of all created realities bear the image and likeness of God, who endowed them with that unique gift (see Gen 1:27). Nevertheless, though Israel stood under divine injunction not to usurp the creative work of God by fashioning idolatrous images of any kind (Ex 20:3–4), its people on numerous occasions did not hesitate to do so. Exodus 32:1–6, for example, recounts how shortly after the covenant was ratified Israel betrayed it by constructing a golden calf to worship in place of the living God. Far from being a purely benign or harmless act, it was anything but, for Israel's worship of an object made by itself actually implied calling a halt to their difficult journey towards the land of hope and liberation, in order to return to the familiar, even though oppressive, situation of slavery in Egypt. As Pablo Richard puts it, 'the sin against the transcendence of God, therefore, consisted in the people's refusal of its own liberation, and in the construction of a false

---

39   See Smith, 'The Glory and Tragedy of Politics', 191–192.

liberation through the alienating worship of a god who would console them, but not set them free'.[40]

No less than the book of Exodus, other books of the Old Testament indicate how Israel, time and time again, constructed useless idols to worship: easily domesticated and undemanding deities, which simply reflected their own human values and aspirations, offered a false sense of security and ultimately victimised the innocent. Against such practices, the prophets of Israel never ceased to berate their people, challenging them to leave idolatry behind and to worship the living God, in whom alone there is salvation (see, for example, Is 44:12–17; Jer 10:1–6). The Wisdom literature recognises that it is not only the ordinary people who fall prey to such folly, as it indicts the ancient sages who idolise the beauty of the cosmos and its processes, failing to recognise them as the handiwork of the divine creator (see Wis 13:1–9). The relevance of this critique continues to endure, as John Courtney Murray makes clear in observing that the error of 'these ancient scientists, ancestors of a long lineage today grown vast in number, ... was to have idolized the pursuit itself', thereby making of their own learning 'the supreme idol'.[41]

In New Testament times, Jesus was no less forceful in challenging his contemporaries to worship the true God, not that 'murderer', the 'father of lies' (Jn 8:44), to whom so many of them gave their allegiance – including those who subsequently conspired to put him to death. Subsequently, St Paul's encounter with the risen Christ on the road to Damascus led him to realise just how wrong his own understanding of God had previously been, as he went about persecuting Christians (see Acts 8:3 and 1 Tim 1:12–17). He also came to see how such a distorted conception still prevailed among his contemporaries, with highly divisive and destructive consequences (see 1 Cor 8:1–13; and Rom 1:18–32).

40   Pablo Richard, 'Biblical Theology of Confrontation with Idols', in Pablo Richard *et al.*, *The Idols of Death and the God of Life: A Theology*, trans. Barbara E. Campbell and Bonnie Shepard (Maryknoll, New York: Orbis Books, 1983) 3–25, at 7.
41   Murray, *The Problem of God*, 83.

In the course of human history, idols and false conceptions of God
have been commonplace, and Christian faith leaves us in no doubt that
the worship of them has resulted in a trail of misery and destruction that
in turn has left countless victims in its wake. Indeed, notwithstanding their
professed commitment to the way of Jesus Christ and to the God of love
he revealed, Christians themselves over the course of time have been far
from blameless in this respect, as instances abound where they turned
'ploughshares' into swords, sanctioned oppressive practices and contributed with zeal to the brutal suppression of those who did not share their
view of God, of Christ, of the Church and of the world. In so doing, they
have shown how relevant is the warning of Jesus himself, that calling out
to him 'Lord, Lord', is no guarantee of authentic Christian discipleship or
worship (see Mt 7:21–27). To that extent, Dawkins and other critics are
perfectly right in highlighting the destructive consequences of religious
fanaticism in its many forms. No less than them, theology too recognises
the need for a hermeneutics of suspicion that cautions against the dangers
of the religious impulse that is misdirected to become merely the 'opium
of the people', with highly destructive consequences. As Bernard Lonergan
makes clear, 'unless religion is totally directed to what is good, to genuine
love of one's neighbour and to a self-denial that is subordinated to a fuller
goodness in oneself, then the cult of a God that is terrifying can slip over
into the demonic, into an exultant destructiveness of oneself and of others'.[42] In brief, idolatrous attempts to domesticate God or Christ have to
be averted in the name of true Christian faith, for they only add to the
misery that afflicts our world.

The God-induced and God-oriented restlessness of the human heart
has already been identified above as constitutive of human existence: a
gift that orients us to transcendence and that calls us to respond by form-
ing right relationships with others and with God. The problem, however,
is that the whole thrust towards transcendence and right relationships
has gone awry, undermined and subverted by the destructive effects of

---

42   Lonergan, *Method in Theology*, 111. See also Haught, *God and the New Atheism*,
      75–77.

sin and evil at work in us and in the world. As a result, our desires and energies are now all too easily misdirected towards relationships that, at best, gratify immediate needs and that, at worst, prove to be immensely destructive of human society and relationships. Even the most pious and ostensibly religious among us are not immune from such tendencies. No less than others, religious believers find it difficult to live with the restless tension at the heart of existence – that 'God-shaped gap' or 'space between'[43] which is both constitutive of human life itself and yet, due to all the sinful conditioning that is our lot, lies beyond our own capacity and effort to negotiate successfully without further sin. Unable to live with that tension, human ingenuity is never found wanting in discovering strategies and ruses to help it cope: by engaging in self-deception; by seeking others on whom to pin the blame for our own inadequacies and failures; and by fashioning deities in our own image that simply strive to eliminate the tension – idols that while promising security and peace of mind, grounded in union with God, merely deliver the illusion of it and inevitably and quickly lead to violence. Some remarks by John Gray on contemporary forms of secularism are certainly apt in relation to these issues: '... secular creeds are formed from religious concepts, and suppressing religion does not mean it ceases to control thinking and behaviour. Like repressed sexual desire, faith returns, often in grotesque forms, to govern the lives of those who deny it.'[44]

The fundamental choice facing every human being, according to René Girard, is not between God and nothing at all but between God and idols of one kind or another.[45] Probing the issue in his anthropological

---

43　This particular image is used by John Caputo; see, for example, *The Weakness of God*, 24, 28 and 122.

44　John Gray, *Black Mass: Apocalyptic Religion and the Death of Utopia* (London and New York: Allen Lane, 2007) 190. Gray argues that the atheism and humanism Dawkins and other militant opponents of Christianity espouse 'are versions of Christian concepts... In affirming human uniqueness in this way, Dawkins relies on a Christian world-view'. Gray, *Black Mass*, 188.

45　See Guido Vanheeswijck, 'Every Man Has a God or an Idol. René Girard's View of Christianity and Religion', in Peter Jonkers and Ruud Welten (eds), *God in France:*

studies, he makes the point that 'humans have always found peace in the shadow of their idols – that is to say, of human violence in a sacralized form. This is still true, as humanity looks for peace under the shelter of the ultimate violence'.[46] The only antidote to such violence, he goes on to argue, is Jesus Christ; he alone reveals both the God of infinite compassion and love who abhors violence, and the religious dynamics of that violence which underpins all human societies and cultures.

In terms of Girard's insights and against the background outlined above, the option is not, as Dawkins would have it, a simple, straightforward one between 'violent religion' and 'peace-loving scientific atheism' underpinned by processes of natural selection that constitute 'a cumulative one-way street to improvement' (141 [169]). On the contrary, the only choice is between the true God and pseudo-gods of every kind; between the way of Jesus Christ that fosters life, leads to truth and brings fulfilment, on the one hand, and the way of self-deception and acquisitiveness that inevitably sanctions and leads to violence, on the other. The choice, in other words, is either the gracious acceptance of the wholly gratuitous gift of love in Jesus Christ, as the only way of fulfilling the God-oriented restlessness of the human heart, or the acquisitive attempt to overcome it by our own grasping, appropriative, selfish and ultimately violent endeavours.

Granted the limited measure of agreement with Dawkins indicated above, therefore, theology quickly draws 'a line in the sand' at it, for along with every hypothetical God and misconceived region 'inhabited by dragons' (374 [419]), he simply eliminates the true God and the entire spiritual realm too. His act of slotting the 'selfish gene' and its ilk into the vacuum thus created constitutes nothing less than idolatry on the grandest scale. In this way, oblivious to the dynamics of the spiritual life, about which he is in complete denial, he proceeds to confirm at least some of those dynamics in quite spectacular fashion. No less than in

---

Eight Contemporary French Thinkers on God (Leuven, Paris, Dudley, MA: Peeters, 2005) 68–95, at 78.

46   René Girard, with Jean-Michel Oughourlian and Guy Lefort. *Things Hidden since the Foundation of the World*, trans. Stephen Bann and Michael Metteer (London: The Athlone Press, 1987) 255.

Augustine's time, 'Felicity' retains its devotees today, though in a variety of ostensibly secular guises such as the 'sexed-up atheism' (18 [40]) and 'the airy and exhilarating freedom' (362 [406]) to which Dawkins gives an enthusiastic nod in the course of his work. Yet there are other deities too, immensely attractive ones before which our contemporaries genuflect; foremost among these is power, the will to which lies at the root of so much trouble in the world.

The Genetic Idol

At this point, it ought to be clear that many of the criticisms of religion put forward by Dawkins are perfectly correct. Religion can have a pernicious influence on human behaviour; it can become an excuse and vehicle for fanaticism of every kind; and it can be highly destructive in its outcomes and its effects. No less than religion, however, numerous secular faiths and ideologies exist that can be equally fanatical, pernicious and destructive: for example, extreme patriotism, fervent nationalism and even atheistic Marxism.[47] In idolising scientific endeavours to the extent that he does and in displacing the Creator God with the selfish gene, however, Dawkins regrettably follows blindly, yet unerringly, that same path. In similar fashion to the aforementioned ideologies, the one he fashions also manifests all the hubris of those who, in the metaphorical terms of the biblical story, sought to reach heaven by their own powers (Gen 11:1–9) and it betrays all the hallmarks of a practice long since exposed by the Scriptures for what it is, namely, idolatry.

In the second chapter of this work, the quasi-religious belief component of Dawkins's approach was identified as a factor to bear in mind in evaluating his stance towards religion. In the third chapter, the ideological character of contemporary scientism was critiqued for the all-embracing nature of its claims that simply cannot be justified on scientific grounds. The relevance of those earlier critiques comes clearly to the fore

47   See Midgley, *Evolution as a Religion*, 17–19.

when the links between ideology and idolatry are examined. That such links exist is implied by the remarks of John Haught that 'scientism and rationalism imprison human minds no less than the worship of idols keeps religious believers from developing a liberating relationship to the whole depth of being'.[48] The links in question have been explored by Bob Goudzwaard, Mark Vander Vennen and David van Heemst in a recent work of theirs.

An analysis of a number of ideologies leads these writers to conclude that, whereas in the past mythology provided a breeding ground for idols to emerge, '*ideology is the matrix, the meaning-framework from which contemporary idols emerge*'.[49] Indeed, according to them,

> the presence of idolatry – the presence of liberating powers designed to make the ideology concrete – serves as the litmus test for determining when the pursuit of a legitimate goal has turned into an ideology. A genuine ideology is present only when some kind of idolatry has taken root in the pursuit of an absolutized end, for only the power generated by the exchange that occurs in idolatry is sufficient to concretely implement an ideology.[50]

Hence, for example, Marxist-Leninism in the Soviet Union constituted one such ideology, where its logic was pushed to the bitter end.[51] In the general terms of this approach, it is arguable that Stalin, despite his professed atheism, was religious and, likewise, so was Hitler. The deities which they worshipped, however, bear no resemblance whatever to, and should under no circumstances be confused with, the Triune God of Christian faith, the Living God who is the Creator and Redeemer of the universe. On the contrary, the deities worshipped wherever tyranny is manifest are nothing but the idolatrous creations of human longings, perverse idols, the worship of which leaves a trail of devastation in its wake.

48   Haught, *God and the New Atheism*, 63–64; see also 75–77.
49   Goudzwaard, Vennen and van Heemst, *Hope in Troubled Times*, 42.
50   Goudzwaard, Vennen and van Heemst, *Hope in Troubled Times*, 42–43.
51   See Goudzwaard, Vennen and van Heemst, *Hope in Troubled Times*, 48–56, where they illustrate their argument and identify six phases of fully developed ideologies.

As already seen in the first chapter, that Darwinian thought can be hijacked for less than salutary ends ought to be clear from the manner in which Social Darwinism was employed by Marxist-Leninists and Nazis in pursuit of their totalitarian objectives. Though obviously he would not condone it, the version of Darwinism espoused by Dawkins seems no less amenable to being hijacked in similar fashion, given his characterisation of religion as a 'virus' and his presentation of extreme, denigrating and fundamentalist readings of the religious standpoint. Much as he would deny it, however, the act of pinning his faith in purely material processes and in the power of scientific reason to comprehend and explain them finally leads him to a dead end: at the 'shrine' of the god of 'ruthless utilitarianism', which in the guise of natural selection 'habitually targets and eliminates waste' and which inevitably 'trumps, even if it doesn't always seem that way' (163 [190–191]).[52]

The history of the twentieth century shows that it requires little imagination to translate that concept 'waste' into human categories and that ruthless individuals and societies are never wanting in devising ingenious ways to eliminate it. Again and again throughout the century, totalitarian regimes of one kind or another spared no effort in targeting, dehumanising and finally eliminating everyone who got in their way: for example, by characterising them as sub-human, as the scum of the earth, as parasites and as vermin.[53] Such regimes were quite ruthlessly utilitarian in pursuing their destructive intent, and they were not slow in claiming Darwin for an ally in so doing. Neither have the various sciences been found wanting in allegiance to the 'idol of power' and pursuing the destructive possibilities inherent in that devotion with religious intensity. In sharp contrast, the God of biblical faith, fully manifest in Jesus Christ, is One who has surrendered power, thereby revealing that real power is both rooted in and perfected by self-giving love.

Christian faith insists that the mystery of Jesus Christ gives definitive expression to God's commitment to the world, which was brought

---

52 See Midgley, *Evolution as a Religion*, 153.
53 See Waller, *Becoming Evil*, 236–257.

into existence not out of necessity or for any need, but simply for love. That awesome love does not overwhelm creation, but rather underpins it, calling forth life and love continuously in the midst of all the turbulence and chaos that characterises it. This insight involves recognition too that in creating God lets go to some extent of the world, allowing it space to be itself and to unfold under the rhythm of its own natural processes.[54] Furthermore, God's ongoing creativity and immanent activity in the natural order, underpinning and upholding it and working ceaselessly through those natural processes to bring forth new life and lead the world to its ultimate destination, are likewise guided solely by love. This clearly involves self-restraint in the exercise of divine power, from which perspective creation is an exercise in divine self-limitation that underpins created freedom and allows for the integrity of natural processes and interactions at every level.[55]

The emphasis on God's self-restraint in dealing with the created order brings to the fore the vulnerability and precariousness of that order, as it unfolds under the guidance of divine love and not by any deterministic programme that sidelines contingency and ignores freedom. Concerning this activity of God in creation, W. H. Vanstone writes:

> Its progress, like every progress of love, must be an angular progress – in which each step is a precarious step into the unknown; in which each triumph contains a new potential for tragedy, and each tragedy may be redeemed into a wider triumph; in which for the making of that which is truly an 'other', control is jeopardised, lost, and, through activity yet more intense and vision yet more sublime, regained; in which the divine creativity ever extends and enlarges itself, and in which its endeavour is ever poised upon the brink of failure.[56]

54   See Haught, *God after Darwin*, 111–114; also Peacocke, 'The Cost of New Life', 23.
55   See, for example, John Polkinghorne, 'Kenotic Creation and Divine Action', 90–106.
56   Vanstone, *Love's Endeavour, Love's Expense*, 62–63.

The existence of evil in the world forces believers to confront the reality of failure in their own lives. Indeed, it brings God face to face with failure too, as the architect of a creative process that hinges on the response of human freedom to divine love. In setting the scene for redemption as an extension of that creative process, however, the inadequacy of freedom's response also becomes the occasion for revealing the extraordinary depths of God's vulnerable love.

Blind to the Self-Effacing God of Jesus Christ

Indeed, were I coerced by the police of orthodoxy into coughing up an argument for the existence of God, I would offer, not a teleological argument, but an ateleological one. I would point to all the disturbances in being and ask, What is the anarchic arche *at the heart of all this disorder? And instead of asking whether some intelligent being must not have designed it, I will ask whether something amorous must not have loved it!*
— JOHN CAPUTO[1]

The light between the ricks of hay and straw
Was a hole in heaven's gable.
— PATRICK KAVANAGH[2]

They make a pit, digging it out,
and fall into the hole that they have made.
— PSALM 7:15

In the course of the previous chapter, it was argued that the act of creation constitutes an enormous risk on the part of God, who in bringing human beings into existence cedes to them the extraordinary gift of freedom, thereby allowing them to forge their own destinies. That gift, however, proves to be an enormous hurdle for the recipients, placing on them a burden they cannot carry and subjecting them to temptations they are unable to resist. Thus sin enters the world to warp human freedom and

---

1   Caputo, *The Weakness of God*, 14.
2   Patrick Kavanagh, 'A Christmas Childhood', *Collected Poems* (London: Martin Brian & O'Keeffe Ltd, 1972 [1964]) 71–72, at 71.

to turn the human heart inwards on itself, thereby leading it to grasp at straws in a manner that subverts the whole thrust to self-transcendence. Thus, too, human relationships are thrown out of kilter and the human condition suffers impairment at every level: at the level of judgment, it continually opts for what strengthens egoism and fosters self-deception at the expense of choosing what is good, true and unifying; at the level of desire, it seeks to satiate its hunger by selfish grasping rather than by an openness to receiving life graciously in all its aspects; and, at the level of freedom, it opts for a highly diluted version of the same that simply understands it as a licence to do whatever it likes, in the illusory conviction that happiness is achievable by human endeavour alone. For Christian faith, the only antidote to this catastrophic state of affairs is a wholehearted turning towards God, who is absolutely central to the entire story of this world and is the key to our lives in it.

The God question cannot be avoided, and one value of *The God Delusion* lies in highlighting that for us. A further value of it, notwithstanding its immense flaws, is its highlighting the prevalence in Western society today of a whole range of distorted images of God that, to put it mildly, are foolish beyond imagining.[3] Though the achievements of Western scientific knowledge are immense, they have been achieved at enormous expense: a theological knowledge that is completely stunted, an infantile understanding of the God in whom 'we live and move and have our being' (Acts 17:28).

The previous chapters of this work have attempted in a small way to grapple with some of the issues that Dawkins raises. Chapter IV utilises the metaphor of the artist in seeking to portray God as the transcendent Creator, whose handiwork is manifest at every level of the created order; the Triune God, constituted by relationality, who created the world and all that is in it for relationality too, to be perfected ultimately in the new

---

3   John Cornwell observes that the image of God advanced by Dawkins falls into the trap of anthropomorphism, whereby God is treated as but a reflection of the human being: '... Your God resembles a Great Big Professor Dawkins in the sky!' John Cornwell, 'A Christmas Thunderbolt for the Arch-enemy of Religion', *The Sunday Times: News Review* (December 24, 2006) 2–3, at 3.

creation in Jesus Christ. Chapter V proceeds from there to highlight God as risk-taker, who identifies with the vulnerability of creation by wagering on human freedom and who comes to bear its burden in the redemptive suffering and death of Jesus on the cross. Now, as this work begins to draw to a close, it is necessary to address more directly Dawkins's misreading of the New Testament in relation to all that Jesus was about: in particular, his charge that the crucifixion of Jesus constitutes 'sadomasochism' of the worst possible kind on the part of God the Father, the brutally vindictive instigator of the death of his own child (see 252 [286]).[4] Far from that being the case, it was not God, but human beings – the Roman state working hand in hand with the religious authorities of Israel – who brought about the death of Jesus.[5] To investigate the reasons for that and to draw out its implications for our study, we need now to reflect on the mysterious character of this God who is ever present to us, but in the most paradoxical and mysterious ways that are not susceptible to human control.

1. The Self-Revelation of God in Jesus Christ

Among the critical points made by Dawkins in the course of his work is the absence of any evidence for God in the events and circumstances of life and of the world. To some extent at least, that is an indictment of Christians themselves, whose witness to the Gospel has not only been sorely lacking but also quite scandalous at times. Hence, as the Second Vatican Council concedes, believers 'have more than a little to do with the rise of atheism'.[6] At the same time, however, what is at stake here goes far

---

4   For other refutations, see Jones, *Challenging Richard Dawkins*, 85–11; Crean, *A Catholic Replies*, 62–94.

5   See Eagleton, 'Lunging, Flailing, Mispunching', 3.

6   Vatican II, *Pastoral Constitution of the Church in the Modern World, Gaudium et Spes* 19; in Austin Flannery (ed.), *Vatican Council II: The Conciliar and Post Conciliar*

beyond the fidelity or otherwise of Christians to the Gospel; it actually goes to the very heart of the faith and comes to a focus in the identity of the God in whom we believe. There are two critical aspects to the issue, necessitating an approach from two sides: through the question of the hiddenness of God, from one side, and through the question of human blindness to God, from the other.

The Hiddenness of God

The basic image of God held by many believers and quite clearly portrayed by Dawkins in the course of *The God Delusion* is that of an activist, interventionist super-being who is ready to jump to attention at every human beck and call. However, as has become painfully clear during the course of human history, that image is fundamentally flawed. Its flaws were perhaps never more apparent than in the course of the last century, most especially in Auschwitz and in the other concentration camps of the Second World War, where the cries for help to God by even the most devout inmates failed to evoke a response. In those places, which can appropriately be designated accursed, God-forsaken and Godless, the evidence for God was entirely lacking. Or was it? For the Christian, the answer to that question is far from straightforward.

The problem of the silence, the hiddenness and the absence of God when people in agony desperately cry for help is a universal problem that poses an immense challenge to religion in every form; for if the claims of religion are true – that the world owes its existence to and is maintained in existence by an all-powerful, benevolent, loving God – then why does God not exercise that power and intervene when most needed? For atheists the answer quite simply is that there is no God; God is at best a projection of human ideals, and so the only response one is likely to hear is

Documents, revised edition (Dublin: Dominican Publications, Leominster: Fowler Wright Books, New Town: E.J. Dwyer, 1987) 903–1001, at 919.

the echo of one's own cries. For believers, however, the answer is far more mysterious, as the biblical approach to the question makes clear.

The inclusion of the Book of Job among the inspired Scriptures is an indication of just how seriously pious believers in Israel struggled with the question of suffering in biblical times. The conventional theological wisdom of the day, articulated by the friends of Job in the course of the book, attributes his suffering to his sinfulness; it is the appropriate divine retribution for the sins he has committed. Though initially Job seems to accept that approach, as the book progresses he grows in the conviction of his own integrity and innocence and defends it vigorously, much to the annoyance of his friends. And, by the book's end, it is Job who is vindicated by God, whose dramatic appearance in the narrative highlights the mysterious nature both of the Creator, who brought this world into existence in a way that far transcends human insight, and of the creation, that continues to be held in the divine care in a way that is far from exhausted by the retributive logic of conventional theological wisdom in Israel. As Gustavo Gutiérrez explains, 'the world of retribution – and not of temporal retribution only – is not where God dwells; at most God visits it. The Lord is not prisoner of the "give to me and I will give to you" mentality. Nothing, no human work however valuable, merits grace, for if it did, grace would cease to be grace. This is the heart of the message of the Book of Job'.[7] Though Job fails to resolve the problem of innocent suffering, the work nonetheless constitutes an invitation, a summons, both to prophecy and contemplation in a mutually support-ive and enriching way: to a prophetic commitment that emphasises the intimate connection between God and all who have to endure unjust suffering in the world, and that struggles to alleviate their plight; and to a contemplative stance that, grounded in the gratuity of God's love, can discern God's presence even in the midst of suffering, thereby eschewing the easy options of apathy and resignation in order to promote resistance to everything that dehumanises.[8]

7   Gustavo Gutiérrez, *On Job: God-Talk and the Suffering of the Innocent*, trans. Matthew J. O'Connell (Maryknoll, New York: Orbis Books, 1987) 88–89.
8   See Gutiérrez, *On Job*, 95.

The reflections on suffering found in the Book of Job reinforce a point that has already been made with respect to the divine action in the world: namely, that hand in hand with God's respect for the integrity of the created world goes God's voluntary self-restraint in all subsequent dealings with it. God freely and lovingly abides by the limitations of the created order in interacting with it at every level, and this is particularly noticeable with respect to the self-imposed limits God places on the exercise of divine power over against human freedom and the constraints of time, even in cases of immense suffering.[9] Indeed, it is nothing short of remarkable that human beings can in freedom resist the divine will, even when that leads to the disfigurement of the beauty and integrity of the created order. The patient, creature-directed love of this timeless God in accepting the burden of history is no less remarkable, but therein for Christian faith lies the mystery that underpins life and the existence of everything in the universe. To a consideration of how the life, death and resurrection of Jesus Christ provide the key to that mystery and give definitive answers to the questions left hanging by Job is an issue to which we must now direct attention.

Manifesting Loving Service unto Death

In the course of his life and ministry around the Galilean countryside, Jesus gradually revealed the face of the God with whom he stood in intimate relationship and addressed as *Abba* (see Mk 14:36): the God of unconditional love, who was entering human history in an unprecedented way and to an unprecedented degree in the life and actions of Jesus himself.[10] That intimate relationship with *Abba* lay behind the revolutionary stance

9   See Haught, *Christianity and Science*, 41–45; and Haught, *God after Darwin*, 52.
10   On the word *Abba* as expressive of everything that Jesus did and said, see John Fuellenbach, *The Kingdom of God: The Message of Jesus Today* (Maryknoll, New York: Orbis Books, 1995) 84; and Eamonn Bredin, *Disturbing the Peace: The Way of Disciples*, third edition (Dublin: The Columba Press, 1991) 37–40.

of Jesus, his 'good news for the poor' that placed God's love for sinners at the very heart of his gospel.[11]

Jesus manifested that love in all his relationships, giving powerful expression to it in his acts of forgiveness and in his table fellowship with sinners of every kind: tax collectors, prostitutes, the ritually unclean and all who were generally designated as impure and held in contempt, according to the religious culture of the day. As a result of associating and even identifying with these religious outcasts on the margins of Jewish society, however, he came to share their impurity and thus to pay a heavy price: religious marginalisation within the community and condemnation by the religious authorities, scandalised by his behaviour.[12] Yet, it is vital to remember why Jesus gave himself so completely in this manner: it was not to boost his own popularity among the people and neither was it to convince the impressionistic and the gullible to follow him; it was rather to expend himself in loving outreach to and commitment to others, even if that meant death.

As the depth of Jesus' commitment to serve and his self-giving in love became clearer to those closest to him, so also their lack of understanding of what he was about increased and their attempts to persuade him to follow another path became more resolute. His family, for example, set out 'to restrain him, for people were saying, "He has gone out of his mind"' (Mk 3:21); Peter rebuked him for his 'defeatist' talk about having to endure great suffering and face death, only to be rebuked even more sharply in return (Mk 8:31–33); and the request by James and John, the sons of Zebedee, for positions of influence and privilege in the kingdom they are convinced he is going to set up, sparked a heated confrontation between them and Jesus' other close disciples, no doubt annoyed because the brothers had pre-empted their own similar requests. In defusing that particular row, Mark reports, Jesus left them in no doubt about what his

---

11   See Bredin, *Disturbing the Peace*, 114.
12   For a brief summary of the ministry of Jesus, see John P. Meier, 'Jesus', in Raymond E. Brown, Joseph A. Fitzmyer and Roland E. Murphy (eds), *The New Jerome Biblical Commentary* (Englewood Cliffs, New Jersey: Prentice Hall, 1990) 1316–1328, at 1320:19.

intent was: 'For the Son of Man came not to be served but to serve, and to give his life a ransom for many' (Mk 10:45).[13]

The extent of Jesus' desire to give his life in service became abundantly clear to the disciples at his last supper with them, when he got down on bended knees to wash their feet, thereby reversing the normal subservience of disciple to master and giving symbolic expression to a way of life where status and prestige count for nothing (Jn 13:14). Shortly afterwards, in the Garden of Gethsemane just prior to his arrest, his unbearable anguish in the face of imminent death is powerfully captured by Mark: 'He took with him Peter and James and John, and began to be distressed and agitated. And he said to them, "I am deeply grieved, even to death; remain here, and keep awake." And going a little further, he threw himself on the ground and prayed that, if it were possible, the hour might pass from him' (Mk 14:33–35). That fearful and agonising experience marked a decisive turning point for Jesus, as his active ministry of inaugurating the kingdom of God came to an end, giving way to his passion in order that the kingdom might somehow be fully realised.[14]

From there, the descent into the abyss of suffering for Jesus was inexorable and rapid. His closest companions were quick to read the signals and abandon him to his fate, with even one of them signalling his betrayal with a kiss (Mk 14:43–52). Handed over to his opponents, Jesus cut a lonely and abject figure, less popular even than the criminal, Barabbas, who was chosen for release by the crowd in preference to him (Mk 15:6–15). Unceremoniously tried by both the religious and political establishments and handed over to Roman military personnel, he met the fate of many a political subversive at the time: torture and execution

13   See Lucien Richard, *Christ: The Self-Emptying of God* (New York/Mahwah, N.J.: Paulist Press, 1997) 69–70; and David N. Power, *Love Without Calculation: A Reflection on Divine Kenosis* (New York: Crossroad, 2005) 25–27.

14   For a brief overview of the attitude of Jesus in facing death, see Thomas P. Rausch, *Who Is Jesus? An Introduction to Christology* (Collegeville, Minnesota: Liturgical Press, 2003) 103–109.

by nailing to a cross.[15] As he hung from it there on Golgotha, an old disused quarry that apparently had its uses as a 'rubbish-dump',[16] his life seemed to have been a complete waste too – of which the bystanders, the passers-by and even his fellow-crucified were not slow to remind him with their mocking and derisory comments (Mk 15:29–32). Even the God to whom he gave allegiance and in whose service he had exhausted himself apparently for nothing finally seemed to desert him too, as he let it be known when crying out in anguish: 'My God, my God, why have you forsaken me?' (Mk 15:34). Though this cry of desolation was somewhat softened by its echoing the opening words of Psalm 22, it brought no deliverance for him there and then. The God to whom he had dedicated his life and with whom he had enjoyed an intimate personal relationship remained silent, apparently disinterested and utterly indifferent to his suffering and death.[17]

The death of Jesus was a brutal affair, an execution sanctioned by the political and religious authorities of the day to rid themselves of one whom they perceived to be a troublemaker of the worst kind – one who preached a message of self-giving love and service and who demonstrated he meant it by actually practising what he preached; one who brooked no compromise in his commitment to the God of infinite love and who communicated that love to all he encountered, regardless of the cost to himself. Hence, notwithstanding the many similarities between the sordid death of Jesus and the executions of numerous others in human history, his death was ultimately different: for he went knowingly and willingly to his death in obedience to *Abba* and in the conviction that his death was

15 See Gerard S. Sloyan, *The Crucifixion of Jesus: History, Myth, Faith* (Minneapolis: Fortress Press, 1995), esp. 18–20.
16 See Wilfrid Harrington, *The Tears of God: Our Benevolent Creator and Human Suffering* (Collegeville, Minnesota: Liturgical Press, 1992) 46.
17 For an exegesis of Mark 15:34, see Raymond E. Brown, *The Death of the Messiah*, Vol. II, *From Gethsemane to the Grave. A Commentary on the Passion Narratives in the Four Gospels* (London: Geoffrey Chapman, 1994) 1043–1056. He finds 'no persuasive argument against attributing to the Jesus of Mark/Matt the literal sentiment of feeling forsaken in the Psalm quote'. Brown, *The Death of the Messiah*, II, 1051.

the key to fulfilling the reality he had ceaselessly proclaimed, the coming of the reign of God.[18] It took a Roman centurion to give voice to the extraordinary depth of the mystery manifest in the event, the presence of God at the very heart of the experience of Godforsakenness: 'Truly this man was God's Son!' (Mk 15:39).

Giving New Sight to the Blind

In beginning his ministry in the synagogue at Nazareth, Luke reports, Jesus interpreted his mission as that of bringing 'good news to the poor', according to the prophetic vision of Isaiah (see Lk 4:16–18; Is 61:1–2). Integral to that mission was the task of giving new sight to the blind. However, it was only in the light of the resurrection and of the presence of the risen Lord to them, as unconditional acceptance and forgiveness and love, that his disciples came to the realisation that they had been among the blindest of all to what he had been about in the course of his ministry.

The resurrection of Jesus from the dead opened the eyes of his disciples to the mystery of his divine identity – he was truly the Son of God – and it enabled them to see clearly for the first time how greatly they had misunderstood him and how deeply they had betrayed him in the events that led to his death on the cross. Gifted with these insights, they now came to understand what they had been incapable of understanding before: that his life was so God-centred and so loving that it rejected no one, even those most opposed to him and to the kingdom that he proclaimed.[19] They came to recognise too that his self-giving unto death was grounded solely in the gratuity of God's love, which he experienced in a uniquely personal and complete way. Jesus, they now understood, had lived with such a total and loving commitment to God and to others

18   See, for example, N. T. Wright, *Jesus and the Victory of God: Christian Origins and the Question of God*, Vol. 2 (London: SPCK, 1996) 540–611.
19   See James Alison, *Knowing Jesus*, second edition (London: SPCK, 1998) 76.

that, in the sinful and violent world we inhabit, 'it was inevitable that he would be crucified'.[20]

As time passed and as their insights deepened, the disciples gave expression to their experience of the Christ-event in the writings that now constitute the New Testament. The theological depth of their reflections comes to clear expression in the Fourth Gospel, where Jesus is presented as the pre-existent Word of God and Son of God, who descended from the Father to enter the world and become one with us so as to redeem us. In this perspective, where Jesus as the embodiment and perfect expression of God's self-giving love is manifestly the light of the world (Jn 8:12), the blindness of his followers becomes starker and more clearcut than ever: for example, in Philip's inability to recognise that whoever has seen Jesus has seen the Father too (Jn 14:8–10) and in Thomas's refusal to believe in the resurrection without direct physical evidence (Jn 20:24–29). The harshest words of Jesus in this Gospel, however, are directed at those who profess to see with perfect vision: the guardians of religious orthodoxy. Having healed the man born blind and restored his vision, Jesus is denounced by them for his act of breaking the law on the Sabbath day (Jn 9). In the ensuing dialogue, Jesus denounces their self-serving blindness in defence of trivialities and delivers his unambiguous judgment on them: '… If you were blind, you would not have sin. But now that you say, "We see," your sin remains' (Jn 9:41).

Human blindness to the glorious light of the resurrection was no less important an issue for Paul, whose encounter with the risen Christ on the road to Damascus cost him his sight for a time, until Ananias laid his hands on him and prayed for him (Acts 9:17–18). His own blindness having thus been dramatically revealed to him, Paul boldly proceeded to proclaim the Gospel of the crucified Christ as 'the power of God for salvation to everyone who has faith' (Rom 1:16). In so doing, he challenged Jews and Gentiles alike to open their eyes widely to the love of God manifest in Christ, and he pleaded with them to respond to that love with love of their own, in order that one day they might share perfectly in it. 'For

---

20   McCabe, *Law, Love and Language*, 133.

now', he writes to the Corinthians, 'we see in a mirror, dimly, but then we will see face to face. Now I know only in part; then I will know fully, even as I have been fully known. And now faith, hope, and love abide, these three; and the greatest of these is love' (1 Cor 13:12–13). In a subsequent letter to the Corinthians, he employed the image of a veil to reinforce his message and to urge them to ever closer union with Christ:

> Since, then, we have such a hope, we act with great boldness, not like Moses, who put a veil over his face to keep the people of Israel from gazing at the end of the glory that was being set aside. But their minds were hardened. Indeed, to this very day, when they hear the reading of the old covenant, that same veil is still there, since only in Christ is it set aside. Indeed, to this very day whenever Moses is read, a veil lies over their minds; but when one turns to the Lord, the veil is removed. Now the Lord is the Spirit, and where the Spirit of the Lord is, there is freedom. And all of us, with unveiled faces, seeing the glory of the Lord as though reflected in a mirror, are being transformed into the same image from one degree of glory to another; for this comes from the Lord, the Spirit (2 Cor 3:12–18).

Thus the plan of God in creating the world is brought to perfect realisation: 'For it is the God who said, "Let light shine out of darkness," who has shone in our hearts to give the light of the knowledge of the glory of God in the face of Jesus Christ' (2 Cor 4:6; see also Eph 1:3–14).

For Paul, though not all can see the glory of the risen Christ – for the minds of unbelievers have been blinded by 'the god of this world' (2 Cor 4:4) – that glory continues to be manifest everywhere, albeit in hidden, mysterious ways through the outpouring of the Holy Spirit; it is manifest most especially in the life of the Church and in the Eucharist, each in its own way the Body of Christ (1 Cor 11:23–26, 12:12–31); it is also manifest in creation itself, which 'waits with eager longing for the revealing of the children of God ...' (Rom 8:19). The challenge for each and for all, then, is to open their eyes to the presence of Christ and their hearts to his love, so that with creation they too may be transformed in him and finally come to share 'the freedom of the glory of the children of God' (Rom 8:21).

As Joseph Ratzinger puts it simply and succinctly, Jesus Christ 'is the definitive human being, and creation is, as it were, a preliminary sketch that points to him'.[21] The God of infinite love has created humanity anew in and through the life, death and resurrection of Jesus Christ. As we have seen, however, human resistance to the ongoing work of God remains a huge factor in life here on earth, as we await the consummation of all things in him. Human blindness to that work continues to be an integral part of that resistance, and so to a brief examination of some of its contemporary manifestations in order to bring this work to a conclusion.

11. A Hole in the Heavens

In bringing *The God Delusion* to a conclusion, Dawkins has recourse to the image of 'the mother of all burkas' (362 [405]) as a way of highlighting the limited nature of human understanding when confronted by the vastness of the cosmos and the mysterious nature of its processes. To express his point another way, our vision of the whole of reality is partial and we are quite myopic in the claims we routinely make to see and understand. This approach to the issue affords us a way of connecting with biblical material once more, in which the person and work of Jesus Christ are pivotal for the Christian.

In the course of the preceding section, Mark 10:45 was identified as a significant biblical verse for approaching the mystery of God's self-emptying love and service in Jesus Christ. The verses immediately following that, detailing the healing of a blind man are no less important for the purposes of this study; for, in identifying the centrality of Jesus Christ for our understanding of the cosmos and of our place in it, they also bring to the fore just how limited our understanding of reality continues to be and how blind we still remain in claiming to see.

21   Ratzinger, *In the Beginning*, 48.

The Blind Cosmologist

All three synoptic Gospels recount a healing miracle by Jesus on the outskirts of the town of Jericho (Mt 20:29–34; Mk 10:46–52; and Lk 18:35–43). Though the details of the event vary in each account, as each of the evangelists situates the event in a particular theological framework and interprets it accordingly, the overall thrust of the message is clear: Jesus, the Son of David, opens the eyes of the blind to the extraordinary power of God now at work in the world through him and about to be fully revealed by his forthcoming passion. Of particular interest to us here, however, is Mark's account for the following reason: unlike the other evangelists and for the only time in the synoptic gospels, the direct beneficiary of the miraculous healing power of Jesus is named; he is Bartimaeus, the son of Timaeus.[22] Though at first glance, the name appears to be without any special significance, Gordon Lathrop argues otherwise, as he draws several parallels between the incident recorded by Mark and one of the classic works of philosophical cosmology, Plato's Timaeus.[23] One key parallel he identifies is the emphasis on sight that is found in each of these texts.

Lathrop highlights how 'the praise of sight' is central to Plato's Timaeus, giving a focus to both its structure and its content. This emphasis on sight 'points both to the scientific basis of his cosmology – observation, followed by deductive reason and mathematics – and to the ethical implications of this cosmological reflection ...'[24] In this vision of things, the philosopher is one who learns to see the divine ways in the orderly movements of the stars and to follow those ways unerringly; by com-

22 For exegetical overviews of the incident, see John P. Meier, *A Marginal Jew*, Vol. II, *Mentor, Message, and Miracles* (New York: Doubleday, 1994) 686–690; and Francis J. Moloney, *The Gospel of Mark: A Commentary* (Peabody, Mass.: Hendrickson Publishers, 2002) 208–211.
23 Gordon W. Lathrop, *Holy Ground: A Liturgical Cosmology* (Minneapolis: Fortress Press, 2003) esp. 25–38.
24 Lathrop, *Holy Ground*, 29.

parison, the lot of the ordinary person as one without sight, completely blind, is to be lamented.

That the issue of sight is no less important in Mark's theological strategy can be gleaned from several incidents that he narrates. At the midpoint of the Gospel, for example, Jesus berates his disciples for their blindness in failing to understand the mystery he has sought to communicate through the miracles he works, most recently in the second miracle of the multiplication of loaves: 'Do you still not perceive or understand? Are your hearts hardened? Do you have eyes and fail to see? ...' (Mk 8:17–18). Against this background, the section immediately following, dealing with the healing in stages of a blind man at Bethsaida (Mk 8:22–26), is quite significant, indicative of a similar healing process taking place at the spiritual level, as the disciples are gradually led to the full vision of who Jesus is: by means of Peter's confession that Jesus is truly the Messiah (Mk 8:27–30); and by the Transfiguration, where the glory of Jesus is revealed to Peter, James and John, even though their understanding of what they see is still partial and flawed (Mk 9:2–8). The process of healing taking place in these incidents is only brought to completion by the centurion's confession of faith upon the death of Jesus on the cross (Mk 15:39), and by his resurrection that guarantees the disciples 'will see him' (Mk 16:7), just as he had previously informed them.[25] This, then, is the wider context in which the healing encounter of Jesus with Bartimaeus outside Jericho takes place and it is a pointer as to how it is to be understood.

In his reading of the incident, Lathrop identifies it as a highly symbolic event that represents a critical encounter between Jesus, 'the son of David', and a follower of Plato, 'the son of Timaeus'. Particularly ironic in this encounter is that whereas Plato in the *Timaeus* highlights and praises the philosophical importance of sight, in the Gospel incident the heir to his philosophy is entirely without sight: 'Here is the "son" of Timaeus, Plato's Timaeus, and, ironically, he is himself blind, crying out in lament,

---

25   See Meier, *A Marginal Jew*, II, 691–692.

seeing nothing, going nowhere'.[26] In sharp contrast to the lot of the blind in the *Timaeus*, however, the cry of the blind in the Gospel is not in vain. For just as he did on the occasion of the aforementioned encounter with a blind man (Mk 8:22–26), Jesus exercises his healing power to restore an individual's sight. The details of the incident as narrated by Mark are again quite illuminating.

Upon hearing from the crowd that Jesus is calling him (Mk 10:49), the first thing Bartimaeus does is throw off his cloak. Though the gesture appears to be wholly innocuous, Lathrop pointedly interjects at this point of his commentary on the text to ask: 'the "philosopher's cloak"? is it philosophy itself that is blind?'[27] Bartimaeus then approaches Jesus and begs him to restore his sight (Mk 10:50–51). On this occasion, the healing takes place instantaneously, as Jesus says to him, '"Go; your faith has made you well." Immediately he regained his sight and followed him on the way' (Mk 10:52). Here again Lathrop insightfully notes that the healing which has just taken place is not merely at the physical level. Bartimaeus has become a believer, who follows Jesus along the way that leads to the cross and the resurrection and who, in so doing, gains a profoundly different insight into the nature of the universe and the view of ethics consistent with it.[28]

For Lathrop, the healing of this man's blindness by Jesus represents for Mark a stunning reversal of Plato's worldview and makes his Gospel a profound contribution to cosmological thought. Though obviously not a complete cosmology, the Gospel text significantly reorients Plato's work by employing 'broken symbols',[29] such as the healing of Bartimaeus, to break through the all-too-neat and perfect scheme of this philosophy. Another example of this disruptive strategy is furnished by the baptism of Jesus, during which Jesus witnessed the heavens themselves being 'torn apart', as the Spirit descended 'like a dove on him' and the Father's voice

26   Lathrop, *Holy Ground*, 31.
27   Lathrop, *Holy Ground*, 32.
28   See Lathrop, *Holy Ground*, 32.
29   Lathrop, *Holy Ground*, 35.

addressed him as 'the Beloved' (Mk 1:10–11).[30] The hearers and readers of the Gospel, who now share this insight into the divine identity of Jesus, recognise that the perfect sphere of the mythic Platonic cosmos is torn open, as the spiritual realm of the Triune God is made manifest here on earth.

In highlighting through the healing of the blind man the inadequacies of the cosmology of the *Timaeus*, Mark's 'broken cosmology'[31] invites his readers to recognise that the deepest and most inclusive cosmological understanding is grounded not in any of our conceptual schemes or symbols, but in the all-embracing mercy of God revealed in Jesus Christ and in his restoration of God's original created order.[32] Though Mark provides numerous possibilities for establishing cosmological connections, the fundamental contours of his own cosmological understanding centre on the salvific outreach of Jesus not only to the blind but also to all who have been ignored, marginalised and trampled upon in this disordered world that stands under a rule other than that of God. In Mark's vision, Lathrop observes, 'the heavens are torn, and the courses of the stars – while belonging to God – are not necessarily the reliable sign of peaceful reason: the sun can be darkened (13:24; compare 15:33), the stars can fall (13:25). Order – deep order for all things – is only to be found in the word and promise of God and in the encounter with the Risen One'.[33]

A Liturgical Cosmology

The encounter with the Risen Christ is decisive for Mark, though at first glance that might not seem obvious, because the accounts of his appearances to the disciples appear to be relegated to an appendix to the Gospel

---

30 For an exegetical commentary on the verse, see Moloney, *The Gospel of Mark*, 35–37.
31 Lathrop, *Holy Ground*, 36.
32 See Moloney, *The Gospel of Mark*, 350.
33 Lathrop, *Holy Ground*, 36.

(Mk 16:9–20), which, scholars inform us, originally ended at Mark 16:8.[34] That original ending describes an encounter at the empty tomb between the women disciples of Jesus and 'a young man, dressed in a white robe', who informs them that Jesus has risen and who instructs them to 'tell his disciples and Peter that he is going ahead of you to Galilee; there you will see him, just as he told you' (Mk 16:7).[35]

Those words of that young man, Lathrop argues, have a far broader application than a purely geographic or historical one; they have a fundamental liturgical orientation too, one that is profoundly relevant to all the disciples of Jesus, including the hearers and readers of the Gospel today, and not just the acquaintances of Jesus himself in those bygone days. That becomes particularly clear when the close association of both healing miracles of the blind with liturgical matters is recognised. After all, the first of those miracles occurs immediately after the spiritual blindness of the disciples has been laid bare by their inability to discern what is at stake in the multiplication of the loaves by Jesus and in the basketfuls of scraps left over (Mk 8:1–10,14–21); and the second of those miracles, the healing of Bartimaeus, follows shortly after Jesus has spoken of his forthcoming death in terms of 'drinking the cup' and of baptism (Mk 10:39). Thus, the coming to see of the two blind men is intimately linked with Jesus' prophecy of his forthcoming death and his pointing to baptism, to the bread and to the cup, as key symbols of that death as the gateway to life in abundance.[36]

Combining these liturgical perspectives with the healings of the blind leads Lathrop to the conclusion that 'Markan cosmology is a liturgical reorientation, not an ideology, not an idea'.[37] In these terms, Mark's Gospel itself is a living text which, when read and pondered in the community of faith assembled for worship today, defines a space under the torn heavens where the risen Christ can actually be encountered in the very act

34   See Moloney, The Gospel of Mark, 354–362.
35   See Moloney, The Gospel of Mark, 348–352.
36   See Lathrop, Holy Ground, 38.
37   Lathrop, Holy Ground, 38.

of reconstituting our world by water and by word, by the breaking of the bread and by the sharing of the cup. Lathrop expresses it as follows:

> The Gospel book itself, read in the assembly, is the resurrection appearance. The whole assembly comes into the hidden meaning of the story, the now manifest, risen identity of the Crucified One. The whole assembly becomes the locus for seeing the torn heavens, receiving the Spirit, hearing the voice of God, being reoriented in the world. Even more, as the text continues, the reader or hearer comes to understand that the fragments of bread from Jesus' great meals (6:30–44; 8:1–10) are still being passed out. Eyes are healed in that shared bread to see the Crucified One as risen. Finally, we see that the way of Bartimaeus, the way of baptism, is open also to us.[38]

To recognise that, however, demands that we recognise our own blindness too and allow the healing power of Jesus to touch our lives and make us whole again.

III. Holes in the Ground

Though approaching the mystery of Jesus Christ and his salvific work from different perspectives, the other writings of the New Testament confirm and support Mark's cosmological vision. Just as 'in him all things in heaven and on earth were created', the letter to the Colossians states, so 'God was pleased to reconcile to himself all things, whether on earth or in heaven, by making peace through the blood of his cross' (see Col 1:15–20). An alternative way of communicating the same message is simply to say that henceforth there is only Christ, who 'is all and in all' (Col 3:11); he is the 'new creation' (2 Cor 5:17) of God, the one in whom all perfection is found and the entire cosmos is destined to share the glory of the resurrection.

---

38   Lathrop, *Holy Ground*, 37.

As we journey onwards through time, however, it is patently clear
that the perfection described by Paul still remains a distant horizon and
that the cosmos still 'groans in labour pains' (Rom 8:22), as it awaits its
glorious transformation. Nevertheless, as Mark's Gospel indicates in highly
symbolic ways, that fulfilment is anticipated here and now in the intimate
union of the Christian community with Christ and demonstrated most
clearly in the liturgy. It is also anticipated and demonstrated in the ongoing commitment of the community to imitate the outreach of Jesus to all
who are marginalised. In this regard, Matthew's Gospel offers us a way of
considering the matter that brings the implications of the cosmological
question to the fore in a slightly different way.

Eruption of Divine Love

In describing the death of Jesus, Mark indicates that immediately after
Jesus had breathed his last, 'the curtain of the temple was torn in two,
from top to bottom' (Mk 15:38), thus precipitating the centurion's confession of faith that Jesus was truly the Son of God. Corresponding to
the hole torn open in the heavens at the moment of Jesus' baptism is the
hole torn in the sanctuary veil of the Temple here on earth.[39] Through
that hole flood the divine blessings by means of which God brings an end
to the Temple cult and transforms all things in Christ.[40]

Matthew's highly symbolic description of the events surrounding
the death of Jesus is similar in most respects to Mark, though with some
changes that are quite illuminating for our purposes here. For one thing,
accompanying the dramatic tearing of the Temple curtain is an earthquake
that splits the surrounding rocks and shakes the earth to its foundations
(Mt 27:51).[41] A similar event takes place in the immediate aftermath of the

39   See Moloney, *The Gospel of Mark*, 328–329.
40   See John P. Meier, *Matthew: New Testament Message* 3 (Dublin: Veritas Publications, 1980) 351.
41   On possible links with ancient cosmologies, see Rudolf Schnackenburg, *The Gospel of Matthew*, trans. Robert R. Barr (Grand Rapids, Michigan: Eerdmans, 2002)

resurrection, when Mary Magdalene and her companion, another Mary, went to visit the tomb: 'And suddenly there was a great earthquake; for an angel of the Lord, descending from heaven, came and rolled back the stone and sat on it' (Mt 28:2). Here again the earthquake signals the shaking of the cosmos to its foundations, as the power of death is overcome and seen to be overcome by the emptiness of the tomb in which the crucified Jesus had lain. That radical transformation is further reinforced by Matthew's disclosure that the representatives of the old imperial and cosmic orders present, the Roman soldiers guarding the tomb, 'became like dead men' (Mt 28:4), upon seeing what had happened.[42] The thrust of Matthew's message is quite clear: the crucified and risen Christ cannot be held in a hole in the ground. The tomb is empty, for the simple and sole reason that in him life has overcome death; he has once and for all overthrown the old established orders, sanctioned by religious authority and backed up by military might with its power to wield death, that put him in that hole in the ground and did their utmost to keep him there.

As we await with Matthew the final consummation of all things in Christ and his future return in glory, we are conscious that the old cosmologies that are underpinned by violence and oriented to death do retain some degree of potency; they can, after all, still engage in deceitful practices that seek to suppress the truth (Mt 28:11–15), and they can still inflict death on the innocent. Nevertheless, their capacity to do so is entirely limited and temporary, for the risen Christ himself leaves us with the assurance of his continued presence among us to the end of time (Mt 28:19). As with Mark, for Matthew that continued presence of Jesus is manifest liturgically in the community and, as the Last Judgment scene depicted by him makes very clear, it is manifest in the actual lives of all those who share his lot on the margins of society: the downtrodden, the excluded and the ignored.

289–290; and R. T. France, *The Gospel of Matthew* (Grand Rapids, Michigan: Eerdmans, 2007) 1079–1081.

42 See France, *The Gospel of Matthew*, 1099–1100; also Meier, *Matthew*, 361.

'Come, you that are blessed by my Father, inherit the kingdom prepared for you from the foundation of the world; for I was hungry and you gave me food, I was thirsty and you gave me something to drink, I was a stranger and you welcomed me, I was naked and you gave me clothing, I was sick and you took care of me, I was in prison and you visited me.' Then the righteous will answer him, 'Lord, when was it that we saw you hungry and gave you food, or thirsty and gave you something to drink? And when was it that we saw you a stranger and welcomed you, or naked and gave you clothing? And when was it that we saw you sick or in prison and visited you?' And the king will answer them, 'Truly I tell you, just as you did it to one of the least of these who are members of my family, you did it to me' (Mt 25:34–40).

The implications of this passage are staggering: the Saviour to whom Christians give allegiance is present in our world among the most unfortunate and despised; the God who out of love for sinful humanity took on human flesh and came to live among us hides in plain sight, among the nobodies and 'good-for-nothings' whom the rest of the world despises. In this light too, the answer to the question previously left unanswered can now be definitively given: God, contrary to all appearances, was in the concentration camps in plain sight too: manifest in the emaciated and the dead, in their embodiment of Christ crucified.[43]

The risen Christ is to be found among the nobodies who count for nothing in a world where other values, such as power and prestige and wealth, hold sway; the layabouts and misfits who have fallen through the cracks in society, which our attempts to paper over only succeed in rendering ever more obvious and dangerous.[44] Mysteriously, however, as Matthew in the above passages indicates, those very cracks render the ground holy, by allowing for the eruption of Christ's power to effect radical changes in society and in the world.

43 See the powerful reflection on the experience of the death of a young child in a concentration camp by Elie Wiesel, *Night*, trans. Stella Rodway (London and New York: Penguin Books, 1981 [1960]) 76–77.

44 See Caputo, *The Weakness of God*, 45.

Fault Lines of Hope

Rooted as we are in a world shaped so decisively by greed and hatred, the power we habitually claim for ourselves over against God and against others is always subject to distortion and its exercise prone to contribute to the violence that makes life miserable for countless numbers of people. Only that love which comes freely as a gift from God in Jesus Christ, to reshape us from within and to renew us in his likeness, can enable us to resist that sinful world and ultimately to transform it in accordance with Gospel values.

The Gospel leaves us in no doubt that at issue here is a power that is manifest more in weakness than in strength, more among the impoverished and oppressed of this world than among the high and mighty, more among the outcasts at the margins of society who are powerless to enforce an agenda of their own than among the rich and influential at the centre who have armies at their beck and call to make things happen. That power is nothing other than the gift of divine love in the ongoing process of redeeming the world, made available and effective by the action of the Holy Spirit and, to put it metaphorically, breaking through the 'fault lines' of our world among the poor and the oppressed, to confound the strong, the arrogant and the self-righteous. In biblical times, those 'fault lines' were centred on Israel, an insignificant and enslaved people, a mere 'worm' (Is 41:14) by comparison with the powerful empires of the world; they ran through Galilee, through Nazareth, about which it was wondered whether anything good could come (Jn 1:46); and they converged finally on the rubbish tip that was an old abandoned quarry outside Jerusalem at Golgotha, where the 'earthquake' of God's love erupted into history (Mt 27:51–54) to effect an extraordinary transformation of the human condition. That too is the power which left the tomb of Jesus empty and which shook his frightened and disoriented followers to such an extent that it transformed them into courageous witnesses who, at no small cost to themselves, risked everything on the name of the one they dared to name 'the Christ'. In their powerlessness, those disciples were touched by most extraordinary power that exists and became channels to communicate it to the entire world.

That same power continues to erupt through the 'fault lines' of the world today where there is least resistance to divine love. It is that same power which underpins the lives of suffering believers everywhere, whose broken bodies witness to the ongoing presence of Christ crucified and risen in a dysfunctional and violent world. That same power too underpins the Church's liturgy, channelled to it by means of ordinary symbols and gestures, words and ritual actions, which by the power of the Holy Spirit become vehicles of divine love for the transformation of the human heart and the entire world in Christ. The drama of divine love that is thus being played out in our midst is cosmic in scope and it is signposted and made effective in a special way in the ritual actions that constitute the sacramental life of the Church. It is mapped out initially for us by baptism, for, as Lathrop reminds us, 'to be baptized is always to be identified with the one who himself identifies with the outsiders and the marginalized'.[45] It is continually deepened by our participation in the other sacraments, and it finds definitive expression in the Eucharist, in which Christ's eschatological transformation of the cosmos, the new creation, is sacramentally re-enacted and anticipated here and now. Far from being a short-cut to redemption, however, that sacramental engagement involves nothing less than a lifelong commitment to discipleship on the part of each and every believer, so that the roots of sin and evil that go deep into the human heart can gradually be removed and life on this earth in its entirety be reconfigured in Christ.

Digging in the Dark

Philosophical cosmologists are blind, or so the reading of the story of the healing of Bartimaeus outlined above would suggest to us. What about their equivalent in other disciplines, such as theology and science? Adopting a theological standpoint and following the insights of Mark and other New Testament writers into the re-creation of all things in the

45   Lathrop, *Holy Ground*, 118.

risen Christ, the temptation to claim perfect vision simply because we are followers of Christ readily beckons. Yet, if the history of Christian thought teaches us anything, it shows us how over and over again it was all-too-easy for Christian thinkers to fall into that trap: defending their clarity of vision when they were actually stumbling about in the dark; claiming to be knowledgeable when all they were demonstrating was ignorance; and throwing their weight about as authoritative experts when all they were doing was acting as bullies. For example, when the Copernican Revolution in cosmology was signalled in the sixteenth century, many Christian thinkers recoiled from the discoveries that had taken place, with the result that the ensuing fallout led to a disastrous split between the natural sciences and theology, from which we are still struggling to recover. To express it once again in metaphorical terms, having confused their own limited grasp of the mystery of divine creation with scientific knowledge, and finding themselves in an unknown place in the cosmos with only outdated maps for guidance, their response bore all the hallmarks of an action cautioned against by the Psalmists: digging a pit and promptly falling into it themselves (see Ps 7:15 and Ps 57:5–6).

Recognition of the folly of our predecessors should be the catalyst for opening our eyes widely to our own limited comprehension in matters of faith, on the one, hand, and on matters of cosmology, on the other. Though the crucified and risen Christ defines the cosmos for Christian believers and though the mysteries of Christian faith in him can be rationally and truthfully expressed by means of doctrines in the manner the Church never ceases to do, our understanding of the entire mystery is still shrouded in obscurity; it is far from exhaustive and it remains partial and open to completion. Christ has transformed the cosmos in its entirety, but, like Bartimaeus, we believers are still blind and in need of healing.

To push the metaphor further, we have to acknowledge how viewing the universe through the lenses furnished by the sciences has greatly improved our vision of the cosmos as a whole and the natural processes taking place within it. The progress that has taken place over recent decades has been nothing short of extraordinary, as it has given us a glimpse of vistas hitherto unimaginable. Intriguingly enough, among the notable scientific discoveries recently made has been one in 2007, by a team of astronomers from the University of Minnesota led by Lawrence Rudnick, of an 'enormous hole' or 'void' in the universe[46] – a region of outer space a billion light years across, which is simply empty, devoid of stars, of galaxies and even of the dark matter that is thus far detectable only by its influence on its visible counterpart in neighbouring regions of space. This discovery, it seems, punches quite a hole too in the standard model of scientific cosmology, as it has been formulated up to now, leaving physicists scrambling for explanations. One explanation postulated thus far is that the hole marks a point of interaction with another universe beyond our own, thus affording us an extraordinary glimpse into the unknown.[47]

Against this background and in the light of the preceding reflections, the words of Lathrop about the various dimensions of scientific inquiry currently being undertaken are worth pondering.

> These are our versions of the *Timaeus*. But all of them have holes, silences, inabilities. None of them should be turned into comprehensive worldviews with an utterly consequent ethics implied. That way lies tyranny. Indeed, the Christian experience of the broken symbol makes a proposal to all worldviews – scientific, religious, philosophical: let them be held critically, with room for lament, room for the other, and room for mercy. Our worldviews – perhaps especially our religious worldviews – are not themselves God. Only one is holy.[48]

46 Reports of the discovery abound on the Internet. See, for example, http://www.reuters.com/article/newsOne/idUSN2329057520070823, and http://www.nrao.edu/pr/2007/coldspot/index.shtml, both accessed on 21 November, 2007.

47 See Marcus Chown, 'Into the Void', *New Scientist* 196/2631 (24 November 2007) 34–37. It is worth noting here how religious imagery can be used by scientists while scientific imagery can be used by theologians. As regards the former, Chown's article contains references to an 'axis of evil' – an unusual alignment observed in the temperature pattern of the early universe, evidenced by current measurements of cosmic background radiation. See Chown, 'Into the Void', 37. As regards the latter, Judy Cannato in her book, *Radical Amazement*, reflects on scientific discoveries from a contemplative standpoint. N. T. Wright also has recourse to this approach in describing evil as 'the moral and spiritual equivalent of a black hole'. N. T. Wright, *Evil and the Justice of God* (London: SPCK, 2006) 72.

48 Lathrop, *Holy Ground*, 36.

And though many of our scientific contemporaries deny it, one alone too, God, has the wisdom and the power to make all things whole and to perfect them in love. That denial has not been without a cost, a quite expensive one too.

For some time now, the dominant cosmological vision of the Western world has been rooted in the knowledge of the world furnished by the sciences. Notwithstanding the enormous successes made possible by this stance towards reality and the 20:20 vision claimed by many of those who adopt it, however, huge blind spots remain, and not just in relation to the fabric of outer space or the nature of infinitesimal particles. They are manifest too in the explicit claims made by those who now think they know it all to supersede every other branch of thought, in the confident dismissal of God as a delusion and in the hubris that for all our evolutionary progress is more entrenched than ever. Thus, unable to see meaning in the universe and to recognise its openness to a truth greater than itself, atheistic scientists have proved themselves to be every bit as adept and obdurate as their theological predecessors in digging, with only the darkness for guide.

Digging is quite an apt metaphor for our times, since much of what we take for granted in contemporary life can be traced to the progress made possible by the ready availability of cheap fossil fuel, oil, literally dug out of the ground. Yet, the diminishing reserves of that precious fuel, combined with the ever-more-apparent effects of burning it as if there were no tomorrow, serve only to bring to the fore the question of limits, to undermine the one-dimensional view of unstoppable progress as it has been conceived, and to suggest in quite graphic terms that the dominant worldview might itself be quite seriously holed. As environmental destruction continues apace and the mountains of waste grow ever higher, as species after species is eliminated and corpse is piled upon corpse, as the rich get increasingly rich and the poor are increasingly impoverished and marginalised, and as planet Earth gets ever more polluted and the precarious nature of our existence on it becomes ever more apparent, the stunted cosmology underpinning the Western vision of unlimited scientific progress has become increasingly apparent to all but those who consider themselves to be the most enlightened.

Though undoubtedly containing much that is beautiful and insightful, worldviews of every sort are seriously flawed too, demonstrating neither innocence nor moral neutrality in respect of key issues concerning life as a whole and humanity in particular. Neither do any of them have an exclusive monopoly on truth, excluding all others and demonstrating perfection and completeness by themselves. As Lathrop suggests, each cosmology is holed, but those holes can also be precious, for a couple of reasons. Firstly, they point to gaps in our knowledge that require us to acknowledge with humility the blindness of our vision and the corresponding stubbornness of our resistance to learn from others. Such an acknowledgement could signal a genuine intellectual conversion, exhibiting a more open stance towards other worldviews and a willingness to learn from them, so as to correct the deficiencies in our own thought. Secondly, and more fundamentally, the holes are precious not as evidence of the blindness of others and not as gaps in human knowledge to be filled by an entirely limited vision of God of our own making projected in ignorance, but rather as channels for a genuine religious conversion through which the power of God that underlies the universe in its entirety – including not only gaps, whenever and wherever they arise, but everything else as well – can erupt to shatter our preconceptions and to expose us to the unlimited love and mercy of God.[49]

As the Gospels of Mark and Matthew demonstrate, there are holes in the Christian cosmos too: a hole in the heavens through which God's word of love can be heard and cracks in the ground through which the power of that same love erupts to transform not only our lives but society and the world in their entirety. In the last analysis, God is love, and its experience of that love commits the Church and its members to a loving response that is integral to the transformation of the world in Christ. Granted that our vision of what he has done is limited, he is still the one who gives sight to the blind (Lk 4:18); and granted that our response to the standards he has set are patently inadequate at times, he too remains the one who opens for us the channels of divine mercy that are always

49   See Lathrop, *Holy Ground*, 44.

available and who assures us that all things will ultimately find their consummation in the love of the Triune God, Father, Son and Holy Spirit.

The Final Word

Creation, the opening chapter of the book of Genesis suggests, can be
understood in terms of a divine utterance or speech act that was uttered
lovingly and gratuitously. The biblical description too presents it almost
as an effortless undertaking on the part of God, the only hint that it
might be otherwise being the well-earned 'Sabbath-day rest' God takes
at the end of the first week. In light of the insights now furnished to us
by scientific endeavours, we now know that that word of extraordinary
creativity, resulting in such an amazing and wondrous universe, first came
to be uttered over thirteen billion years ago.

Endowed with the capacity for language and words, human beings are
capable of probing the mystery of creation in varied and insightful ways.
Such is the vastness and depth of that mystery, however, that in the face
of it all the words ever uttered and capable of being uttered are barely able
to probe its surface layers, thereby rendering an exhaustive description of
the entire mystery far beyond our reach and endeavours.

For Christian faith, nonetheless, that is not the end of the story,
because every moment of time from the beginning was prelude to an even
more significant speech act, involving preparation and groundwork that
was extraordinarily intricate and detailed, yet always contingent and free
too: God's complete and total self-utterance in the Incarnation of Jesus
Christ.[50] From the expenditure of vast amounts of energy at the macro
level, generated by the Big Bang and leading to the emergence of stars
and galaxies in the farthest reaches of the universe, to the tiniest and most
intricate movements of highly elusive particles at the quantum level, everything unfolded in a manner appropriate to the natural scheme of things
set in place under the watchful eye of its loving Creator. The evolution

50   See Ratzinger, *On the Way to Jesus Christ*, 82–83.

of life itself, by complex and elaborate processes, and the emergence of consciousness and language, by which to decipher and understand those processes, were intrinsic elements of that detail, as the Creator prepared the way for the coming to be of the Word made flesh. For reasons that are wholly mysterious and beyond our grasp, because they pertain to the Triune God alone, creation was destined to be the ground for creaturely communion in freedom with the Creator.

The Incarnation of the Word is not the end of the story either, because creaturely freedom rejected God's invitation to communion out of hand, exacting a terrible price on Jesus Christ, its bearer and living manifestation, in so doing. Hence, though the biblical account of creation presents it as an effortless endeavour on the part of God who created everything 'out of nothing', the biblical account of God's re-creation of all things out of the corpse of Jesus Christ, the Incarnate Son, leaves believers in no doubt whatever about its cost.[51] The Sabbath rest thus points to the vulnerability of the Creator's love, on which rests the entirety of creation in all its precariousness and by which it is ultimately redeemed. Totally committed to creation and yet powerless in the face of the freedom voluntarily surrendered and bestowed wholly gratuitously on it, God exposes the divine love to the utmost limit in bearing the burden of and ultimately subverting humankind's sinful 'no' with an inexhaustible, loving 'yes' that resounds through the cosmos (see 2 Cor 1:18–22). The theology of creation indicates quite clearly that God underpins the whole of creation and every facet of it; the theology of redemption indicates no less clearly that God, having assumed the burden of creation, ensures its redemption by plumbing it to the dregs with a love that is both breathtaking and limitless.[52]

Though the work of the Redeemer is complete and the re-creation of the cosmos in its entirety has already been effected by his resurrection, it remains for us to make it our own and to make our own tiny contribution to it in creative freedom. As we journey towards the consummation

51   See Denis Carroll, *Towards a Story of the Earth* (Dublin: Dominican Publications, 1987) 34–35.
52   See Vanstone, *Love's Endeavour, Love's Expense*, 72.

of all things in Christ, therefore, God's creative project is ongoing. God still speaks, never ceasing to issue the invitation to make our home in the world in a way that is faithful to the definitive Word of love, Jesus Christ himself.

To conclude, it is worth recalling the point made by B. W. Anderson that 'creation is fundamentally an eschatological doctrine'.[53] Paul Ricoeur reinforces the thrust of that position, when he argues that 'the always-already-there of Creation does not make sense independently of the perpetual futurity of Redemption. Between these two is intercalated the eternal now of the "you, love me!"'[54] That divine summons indicates that the entire cosmos, together with everything that has ever happened in it, stands under the 'eternal now' of God's love. Hence, nothing that ever happened in the created world has ever been lost to God: every movement of every particle, every manifestation and expenditure of energy, every second of every cell and every ounce of sweat expended by every living creature in its time here in the realm of creation, have all unfolded under the love of God. And, at the moment of consummation, when history will be complete, they will find their completion too, perfected with all creation in the fullness of divine love when God will be 'all in all' (1 Cor 15:28).[55]

53　Quoted by LaCoque, 'Cracks in the Wall', 7; original in B. W. Anderson, 'Creation', *Interpreter's Dictionary of the Bible* (New York: Abingdon, 1962) Vol. 1, 730.

54　Ricoeur, 'Thinking Biblically', 67.

55　See Vatican II, *Gaudium et Spes* 39, in Flannery (ed.), *Vatican Council II*, 938.

Bibliography

Scripture quotations are from the *New Revised Standard Version* of the Bible.

Alison, James. *The Joy of Being Wrong: Original Sin through Easter Eyes.* New York: The Crossroad Publishing Company, 1998.
—— *Knowing Jesus.* Second edition. London: SPCK, 1998.
—— *Faith beyond Resentment: Fragments Catholic and Gay.* London: Darton, Longman & Todd, 2001.
Arendt, Hannah. *The Origins of Totalitarianism.* New York: Schocken Books, 2004 [1948].
Barron, Robert. *Thomas Aquinas: Spiritual Master.* New York: The Crossroad Publishing Company, 1996.
Barry, Patrick. 'What's Done Is Done ...' *New Scientist* 191/2571 (30 September 2006) 36–39.
Baumgartner, Frederick J. *Longing for the End: A History of Millennialism in Western Culture.* New York: St Martin's Press, 1999.
Beattie, Tina. *The New Atheists: The Twilight of Reason and the War on Religion.* London: Darton, Longman & Todd, 2007.
Berry, Thomas. *The Dream of the Earth.* San Francisco: Sierra Club Books, 1988.
Bostrom, Nick. 'Do We Live in a Computer Simulation?' *New Scientist,* 50th Anniversary Special 1956–2006, 192/2578 (18 November 2006) 38–39.
Boureux, Christophe, and Christoph Theobald, eds. *Original Sin: A Code of Fallibility. Concilium* (2004/1).
Bredin, Eamonn. *Disturbing the Peace: The Way of Disciples.* Third edition. Dublin: The Columba Press, 1991.
Broks, Paul. 'What is Consciousness?' *New Scientist,* 50th Anniversary Special 1956–2006, 192/2578 (18 November 2006) 56–61.

Brooks, Michael. 'In Place of God'. *New Scientist*, 50th Anniversary Special 1956–2006, 192/2578 (18 November 2006) 8–11.

Brown, Raymond E. *The Death of the Messiah*, Volume II, *From Gethsemane to the Grave. A Commentary on the Passion Narratives in the Four Gospels*. London: Geoffrey Chapman, 1994.

Bruteau, Beatrice. *God's Ecstasy: The Creation of a Self-Creating World*. New York: The Crossroad Publishing Company, 1997.

Burleigh, Michael. *Sacred Causes: Religion and Politics from the European Dictators to Al Qaeda*. London: HarperPress, 2006.

Burrell, David B. 'Act of Creation with Its Theological Consequences'. In Thomas Weinandy, Daniel Keating and John Yocum, eds. *Aquinas on Doctrine: A Critical Introduction*. London and New York: T & T Clark, 2004, 27–44.

Butterfield, Herbert. *Christianity and History*. London and Glasgow: Collins Fontana Books, 1957 [1949].

Cannato, Judy. *Radical Amazement: Contemplative Lessons from Black Holes, Supernovas, and Other Wonders of the Universe*. Notre Dame, Indiana: Sorin Books, 2006.

Capra, Fritjof. *The Turning Point: Science, Society, and the Rising Culture*. Toronto: Bantam Books, 1982.

Caputo, John D. *The Weakness of God: A Theology of the Event*. Bloomington and Indianapolis: Indiana University Press, 2006.

Carroll, Denis. *Towards a Story of the Earth*. Dublin: Dominican Publications, 1987.

Chown, Marcus. 'Forever Quantum'. *New Scientist* 193/2595 (17 March 2007) 36–39.

—— 'Into the Void'. *New Scientist* 196/2631 (24 November 2007) 34–37.

Close, Frank. *The Void*. Oxford and New York: Oxford University Press, 2007.

Cornwell, John. *Darwin's Angel: A Seraphic Response to* The God Delusion. London: Profile Books, 2007.

—— 'A Christmas Thunderbolt for the Arch-enemy of Religion'. *The Sunday Times: News Review* (24 December 2006) 2–3.

Crean, Thomas. *A Catholic Replies to Professor Dawkins*. Oxford: Family Publications, 2007.

Davies, Oliver. *The Creativity of God: World, Eucharist, Reason*. Cambridge and New York: Cambridge University Press, 2004.

Davies, Paul. *The Goldilocks Enigma: Why Is the Universe Just Right for Life?* London and New York: Allen Lane, 2006.

Dawkins, Richard. *The Selfish Gene*. Second edition. Oxford and New York: Oxford University Press, 1989 [1976].

—— *River out of Eden: A Darwinian View of Life*. London: Phoenix, 1995.

—— *Unweaving the Rainbow: Science, Delusion and the Appetite for Wonder*. London and New York: Penguin Books, 1998.

—— *The God Delusion*. London: Bantam Press, 2006.

—— *The God Delusion*. Second edition. London: Black Swan, 2007.

Dennett, Daniel C. *Consciousness Explained*. London and New York: Allen Lane. The Penguin Press, 1991.

—— *Darwin's Dangerous Idea: Evolution and the Meanings of Life*. London and New York: Penguin Books, 1995.

Duffy, Stephen J. 'Our Hearts of Darkness: Original Sin Revisited'. *Theological Studies* 49/4 (October 1988) 597–622.

—— *The Dynamics of Grace: Perspectives in Theological Anthropology*. Collegeville, Minnesota: The Liturgical Press, 1993.

Dussel, Enrique. *History and the Theology of Liberation: A Latin American Perspective*. Translated by John Drury. Maryknoll, New York: Orbis Books, 1976.

Dyson, Freeman. 'Our Biotech Future'. *The New York Review of Books* LIV/12 (19 July 2007) 4, 6, 8.

Edwards, Denis. *The God of Evolution: A Trinitarian Theology*. New York/Mahwah, N.J.: Paulist Press, 1999.

—— *Ecology at the Heart of Faith: The Change of Heart that Leads to a New Way of Living on Earth*. Maryknoll, New York: Orbis Books 2006.

Egan, Joe. *Brave Heart of Jesus: Mel Gibson's Postmodern Way of the Cross*. Dublin: The Columba Press, 2004.

Flannery, Austin, gen. ed. *Vatican Council II: The Conciliar and Post Conciliar Documents*. Revised edition. Dublin: Dominican Publications, Leominster: Fowler Wright Books Ltd. and Sydney: E.J. Dwyer Pty. Ltd., 1988.

France, R. T. *The Gospel of Matthew*. Grand Rapids, Michigan: William B. Eerdmans Publishing Company, 2007.

Frankl, Viktor E. *Man's Search for Meaning: An Introduction to Logotherapy*. Translated by Ilse Lasch. London: Hodder and Stoughton, 1964 [1962].

Fretheim, Terence E. *God and the World in the Old Testament: A Relational Theology of Creation*. Nashville: Abingdon Press, 2005.

Fromm, Erich. *The Fear of Freedom*. London: Routledge and Kegan Paul Ltd., 1960 [1942].

Fuellenbach, John. *The Kingdom of God: The Message of Jesus Today*. Maryknoll, New York: Orbis Books, 1995.

Girard, René, with Jean-Michel Oughourlian and Guy Lefort. *Things Hidden since the Foundation of the World*. Translated by Stephen Bann and Michael Metteer. London: The Athlone Press, 1987.

Goudzwaard, Bob, Mark Vander Vennen and David van Heemst. *Hope in Troubled Times: A New Vision for Confronting Global Crises*. Grand Rapids, Michigan: Baker Academic, 2007.

Gray, John. *Heresies: Against Progress and Other Illusions*. London: Granta Books, 2004.

—— *Black Mass: Apocalyptic Religion and the Death of Utopia*. London and New York: Allen Lane, 2007.

—— 'The Atheist Delusion'. *The Guardian: Review* (Saturday, 15 March, 2008) 4–6.

Greene, Colin J. D. *Christology in Cultural Perspective: Marking out the Horizons*. Grand Rapids, Michigan, and Cambridge, U.K.: William B. Eerdmans Publishing Company, 2003.

Groppe, Elizabeth T. 'Creation *ex nihilo* and *ex amore*: Ontological Freedom in the Theologies of John Zizioulas and Catherine Mowry LaCugna'. *Modern Theology* 21/3 (July 2005) 463–496.

Gutiérrez, Gustavo. *On Job: God-Talk and the Suffering of the Innocent.* Translated by Matthew J. O'Connell. Maryknoll, New York: Orbis Books, 1987.

Harrington, Wilfrid. *The Tears of God: Our Benevolent Creator and Human Suffering.* Collegeville, Minnesota: The Liturgical Press, 1992.

Haught, John F. *God after Darwin: A Theology of Evolution.* Boulder, Colorado, and Oxford: Westview Press, 2000.

―― *Christianity and Science: Toward a Theology of Nature.* Maryknoll, New York: Orbis Books, 2007.

―― *God and the New Atheism: A Critical Response to Dawkins, Harris, and Hitchens.* Louisville, Kentucky, and London: Westminster John Knox Press, 2008.

Hayes, Zachary. *The Gift of Being: A Theology of Creation.* Collegeville, Minnesota: The Liturgical Press, 2001.

Hazen, Robert. 'What Is Life?' *New Scientist,* 50th Anniversary Special 1956–2006, 192/2578 (18 November 2006) 46–51.

Hick, John. *The New Frontier of Religion and Science: Religious Experience, Neuroscience and the Transcendent.* Houndmills, U.K., and New York: Palgrave Macmillan, 2006.

Hind, Dan. *The Threat to Reason: How the Enlightenment Was Hijacked and How We Can Reclaim It.* London and New York: Verso, 2007.

Johnson, Elizabeth A. 'Does God Play Dice? Divine Providence and Chance'. *Theological Studies* 57/1 (March 1996) 3–18.

―― *Quest for the Living God: Mapping Frontiers in the Theology of God.* New York and London: The Continuum International Publishing Group Inc., 2007.

Jones, Kathleen. *Challenging Richard Dawkins: Why Richard Dawkins Is Wrong about God.* Norwich: Canterbury Press, 2007.

Kaku, Michio. 'Will We Ever Have a Theory of Everything?' *New Scientist,* 50th Anniversary Special 1956–2006, 192/2578 (18 November 2006) 62–65.

Kasper, Walter. *The God of Jesus Christ.* Translated by Matthew J. O'Connell. London: SCM Press Ltd., 1983.

Kavanagh, Patrick. *Collected Poems*. London: Martin Brian & O'Keeffe Ltd, 1972 [1964].

Keller, Catherine. *Face of the Deep: A Theology of Becoming*. London and New York: Routledge, 2003.

Kelly, Tony. *An Expanding Theology: Faith in a World of Connections*. Newtown, NSW: E. J. Dwyer, 1993.

Kerr, Fergus. *After Aquinas: Versions of Thomism*. Malden, MA, and Oxford, U.K.: Blackwell Publishing, 2002.

—— *Twentieth-Century Catholic Theologians: From Neoscholasticism to Nuptial Mysticism*. Malden, MA, and Oxford, U.K.: Blackwell Publishing, 2007.

Küng, Hans. *The Beginning of All Things. Science and Religion.* Translated by John Bowden. Grand Rapids, Michigan, and Cambridge, U.K.: William B. Eerdmans Publishing Company, 2005.

Lash, Nicholas. 'Where Does *The God Delusion* Come from?' *New Blackfriars* 88/1017 (September 2007) 507–521.

—— *Theology for Pilgrims*. London: Darton, Longman & Todd, 2008.

LaCoque, André, and Paul Ricoeur. *Thinking Biblically: Exegetical and Hermeneutical Studies*. Translated by David Pellauer. Chicago and London: University of Chicago Press, 1998.

LaCugna, Catherine Mowry. *God for Us: The Trinity and Christian Life*. San Francisco: HarperSanFrancisco, 1991.

Lathrop, Gordon W. *Holy Ground: A Liturgical Cosmology*. Minneapolis, MN: Fortress Press, 2003.

Lonergan, Bernard J. F. *Insight: A Study of Human Understanding*. Third edition. New York: Philosophical Library, 1970.

—— *Grace and Freedom: Operative Grace in the Thought of St. Thomas Aquinas*. Edited by J. Patout Burns. New York: Herder and Herder, 1971.

—— *Method in Theology*. Toronto: University of Toronto Press, 1971.

—— *A Second Collection*. Edited by William F. J. Ryan and Bernard J. Tyrrell. London: Darton, Longman & Todd, 1974.

Mackey, James P. *Christianity and Creation: The Essence of the Christian Faith and Its Future among Religions*. New York and London: The Continuum International Publishing Group Inc., 2006.

—— *The Scientist and the Theologian: On the Origin and Ends of Creation*. Dublin: The Columba Press, 2007.

Marsh, Thomas. *The Triune God: A Biblical, Historical and Theological Study*. Dublin: The Columba Press, 1994.

McCabe, Herbert. *Law, Love and Language*. London and New York: The Continuum International Publishing Group Inc., 2003 [1968].

McCool, Gerald A. *From Unity to Pluralism: The Internal Evolution of Thomism*. New York: Fordham University Press, 1989.

McGrath, Alister E. *A Scientific Theology*, Volume 1, *Nature*. Edinburgh: T & T Clark, 2001.

—— *A Scientific Theology*, Volume 2, *Reality*. Edinburgh and New York: T & T Clark, 2002.

—— *A Scientific Theology*, Volume 3, *Theory*. Grand Rapids, Michigan: William B. Eerdmans Publishing Company, 2003.

—— *Dawkins' God: Genes, Memes, and the Meaning of Life*. Malden, MA, and Oxford: Blackwell Publishing, 2005.

McGrath, Alister, with Joanna Collicutt McGrath. *The Dawkins Delusion: Atheist Fundamentalism and the Denial of the Divine*. London: SPCK, 2007.

Meier, John P. *Matthew: New Testament Message 3*. Dublin: Veritas Publications, Wilmington, Delawere: Michael Glazier, Inc., 1980.

—— 'Jesus'. In Raymond E. Brown, Joseph A. Fitzmyer and Roland E. Murphy, eds. *The New Jerome Biblical Commentary*. Englewood Cliffs, New Jersey: Prentice Hall, 1990, 1316–1328.

—— *A Marginal Jew*, Volume II, *Mentor, Message, and Miracles*. New York: Doubleday, 1994.

Midgley, Mary. *Science as Salvation: A Modern Myth and Its Meaning*. London and New York: Routledge, 1992.

—— *Evolution as a Religion: Strange Hopes and Stranger Fears*. Second edition. London and New York: Routledge, 2002.

—— *The Myths We Live By*. London and New York: Routledge, 2004.

—— *Science and Poetry*. Second edition. London and New York: Routledge, 2006 [2001].

Min, Anselm K. *Paths to the Triune God: An Encounter between Aquinas and Recent Theologies*. Notre Dame, Indiana: University of Notre Dame Press, 2005.

Moloney, Francis J. *The Gospel of Mark: A Commentary*. Peabody, Mass.: Hendrickson Publishers, 2002.

Moltmann, Jürgen. *God and Creation: An Ecological Doctrine of Creation*. London: SCM Press Ltd., 1985.

Monod, Jacques. *Chance and Necessity: An Essay on the Natural Philosophy of Modern Biology*. Translated by Austryn Wainhouse. London: Collins, 1972.

Morales, José. *Creation Theology*. Dublin and Portand, OR: Four Courts Press, 2001.

Murray, John Courtney. *The Problem of God: Yesterday and Today*. New Haven and London: Yale University Press, 1964.

Nichols, Terence L. *The Sacred Cosmos: Christian Faith and the Challenge of Naturalism*. Grand Rapids, Michigan: Brazos Books, 2003.

O'Collins, Gerald. *Jesus Risen: The Resurrection – What Actually Happened and What Does It Mean?* London: Darton, Longman & Todd, 1987.

—— *The Tripersonal God: Understanding and Interpreting the Trinity*. London: Geoffrey Chapman, 1999.

O'Donnell, John J. *The Mystery of the Triune God*. London: Sheed & Ward Ltd., 1988.

O'Malley, William J. *God: The Oldest Question*. Chicago: Loyola Press, 2000.

Ó'Murchú, Diarmuid. *Quantum Theology: Spiritual Implications of the New Physics*. New York: The Crossroad Publishing Company, 1997.

Ormerod, Neil. 'Chance and Necessity, Providence and God'. *The Irish Theological Quarterly* 70/3 (2005) 263–278.

—— *Creation, Grace, and Redemption*. Maryknoll, New York: Orbis Books, 2007.

Pannenberg, Wolfhart. *Faith and Reality*. Translated by John Maxwell. London: Search Press, Philadelphia: The Westminster Press, 1977.

—— *Toward a Theology of Nature: Essays on Science and Faith*. Edited by Ted Peters. Louisville, Kentucky: Westminster/John Knox Press, 1993.

Peacocke, Arthur. *Creation and the World of Science: The Re-Shaping of Belief*. Oxford: Oxford University Press, 2004.

Penrose, Roger. 'What is Reality?' *New Scientist*, 50th Anniversary Special 1956–2006, 192/2578 (18 November 2006) 32–39.

Polkinghorne, John, ed. *The Work of Love: Creation as Kenosis*. Grand Rapids, Michigan: William B. Eerdmans Publishing Company, London: SPCK, 2001.

Polkinghorne, John. *Science and the Trinity: The Christian Encounter with Reality*. London: SPCK, 2004.

—— *One World: The Interaction of Science and Theology*. Philadelphia and London: Templeton Foundation Press, 2007 [1986].

—— *Quantum Physics and Theology: An Unexpected Kinship*. London: SPCK, 2007.

Polanyi, Michael. *Personal Knowledge: Towards a Post-Critical Philosophy*. London, Melbourne and Henley: Routledge and Kegan Paul 1973 [1958].

Porter, Jean. *Nature as Reason: A Thomistic Theory of the Natural Law*. Grand Rapids, Michigan: William B. Eerdmans Publishing Company, 2005.

Powell, Corey S. *God in the Equation: How Einstein Transformed Religion*. New York, London, Toronto, Sydney, Free Press, 2002.

Power, David N. *Love Without Calculation: A Reflection on Divine Kenosis*. New York: The Crossroad Publishing Company, 2005.

Prusak, Bernard P. 'Bodily Resurrection in Catholic Perspectives'. *Theological Studies* 61/1 (March 2000) 64–105.

Ratzinger, Joseph. *Eschatology: Death and Eternal Life*. Translated by Michael Waldstein. Translation edited by Aidan Nichols. Washington, D.C.: The Catholic University of America Press, 1988.

—— *In the Beginning: A Catholic Understanding of the Story of Creation and the Fall*. Translated by Boniface Ramsey. Edinburgh: T & T Clark, 1990.

—— *On the Way to Jesus Christ*. Translated by Michael J. Miller. San Francisco: Ignatius Press, 2005.

____ Pope Benedict XVI. *Spe Salvi: Encyclical Letter on Christian Hope*. London: Catholic Truth Society, 2007.

Rausch, Thomas P. *Who Is Jesus? An Introduction to Christology*. Collegeville, Minnesota: The Liturgical Press, 2003.

Richard, Lucien. *Christ: The Self-Emptying of God*. New York/Mahwah, N.J.: Paulist Press, 1997.

Richard, Pablo *et al*. *The Idols of Death and the God of Life: A Theology*. Translated by Barbara E. Campbell and Bonnie Shepard. Maryknoll, New York: Orbis Books, 1983.

Ricoeur, Paul. *The Symbolism of Evil*. Translated by Emerson Buchanan. Boston: The Beacon Press, 1969.

Scheffczyk, Leo. *Creation and Providence*. Translated by Richard Strachan. New York: Herder and Herder, London: Burns & Oates, 1970.

Schnackenburg, Rudolf. *The Gospel of Matthew*. Translated by Robert R. Barr. Grand Rapids, Michigan: William B. Eerdmans Publishing Company, 2002.

Schwartz, Ronald B., ed. *The Best Things Ever Said about God*. New York: Quill, 2000.

Shorter, Aylward. *Revelation and Its Interpretation*. London: Geoffrey Chapman, 1983.

Siegelbaum, Lewis, and Andrei Sokolov. *Stalinism as a Way of Life: A Narrative in Documents*. Abridged Edition. Translated by Steven Shabad and Thomas Hoisington. New Haven and London: Yale University Press, 2004.

Sloyan, Gerard S. *The Crucifixion of Jesus: History, Myth, Faith*. Minneapolis, MN: Fortress Press, 1995.

Smith, Thomas W. 'The Glory and Tragedy of Politics'. In John Doody, Kevin L. Hughes, and Kim Paffenroth, eds. *Augustine and Politics*. Lanham, Maryland: Lexington Books, 2005, 187–213.

Soelle, Dorothee. *The Mystery of Death*. Translated by Nancy Lukens-Rumscheidt and Martin Lukens-Rumscheidt. Minneapolis, MN: Fortress Press, 2007.

St Augustine, *The Trinity*. Translated by Edmund Hill. Edited by John
E. Rotelle. Brooklyn, New York: New City Press, 1991.
—— 'Sermon 126'. In *Sermons. The Works of Saint Augustine: A Translation
for the 21st Century*, Volume III/4. Translated by Edmund Hill. Edited
by John E. Rotelle. Brooklyn, New York: New City Press, 1992.
—— *Confessions*. Translated by Henry Chadwick. Oxford and New York:
Oxford University Press, 1992.
—— *City of God*. Translated by Henry Bettenson. London: Penguin
Books, 2003 [1972].
Steiner, George. *Real Presences*. Chicago: University of Chicago Press,
London: Faber and Faber, 1989.
—— *Grammars of Creation*. London: Faber and Faber, 2001.
Stump, Eleonore. *Aquinas*. London and New York: Routledge, 2003.
Tarnas, Richard. *The Passion of the Western Mind: Understanding the Ideas
that Have Shaped Our World View*. London: Pimlico, 1991.
Teilhard de Chardin, Pierre. *The Hymn of the Universe*. London: William
Collins Sons and Co. Ltd., 1965.
Toom, Tarmo. *Classical Trinitarian Theology: A Textbook*. New York and
London: T & T Clark, 2007.
Torrell, Jean-Pierre. *Saint Thomas Aquinas*. Volume 2, *Spiritual Master*.
Translated by Robert Royal. Washington, D.C.: The Catholic
University of America Press, 2003.
Tracy, David. *Blessed Rage for Order: The New Pluralism in Theology*.
Minneapolis, MN: The Winston – Seabury Press, 1975.
Turner, Denys. *Faith Seeking*. London: SCM Press Ltd., 2002.
Vanheeswijck, Guido. 'Every Man Has a God or an Idol. René Girard's
View of Christianity and Religion'. In Peter Jonkers and Ruud
Welten, eds. *God in France: Eight Contemporary French Thinkers on
God*. Leuven, Paris, and Dudley, MA: Peeters, 2005, 68–95.
Vanstone, W. H. *Love's Endeavour, Love's Expense: The Response of Being
to the Love of God*. London: Darton, Longman & Todd, 1977.
Vedral, Vlatko. 'Is the Universe Deterministic?' *New Scientist*, 50th
Anniversary Special 1956–2006, 192/2578 (18 November 2006)
52–55.

von Balthasar, Hans Urs. *The Glory of the Lord: A Theological Aesthetics.* Volume I, *Seeing the Form.* Translated by Erasmo Leiva-Merikakis. Edited by John Riches. Edinburgh: T & T Clark, 1982.

—— *Theo-Drama: Theological Dramatic Theory*, Volume II, *Dramatis Personae: Man in God.* Translated by Graham Harrison. San Francisco: Ignatius Press, 1990.

—— *Theo-Drama: Theological Dramatic Theory*, Volume IV, *The Action.* Translated by Graham Harrison. San Francisco: Ignatius Press, 1994.

—— *Theo-Drama: Theological Dramatic Theory*, Volume V, *The Last Act.* Translated by Graham Harrison. San Francisco: Ignatius Press, 1998.

Waller, James. *Becoming Evil: How Ordinary People Commit Genocide and Mass Killing.* Oxford and New York: Oxford University Press, 2002.

Ward, Keith. *Pascal's Fire: Scientific Faith and Religious Understanding.* Oxford: Oneworld Publications, 2006.

—— *The Big Questions in Science and Religion.* West Conshohocken, Pennsylvania: Templeton Foundation Press, 2008.

—— *Why There Almost Certainly Is a God: Doubting Dawkins.* Oxford: Lion Hudson plc, 2008.

Wiener, Linda, and Ramsey Eric Ramsey. *Leaving Us to Wonder: An Essay on the Questions Science Can't Ask.* Albany, New York: State University of New York Press, 2005.

Wiesel, Elie. *Night.* Translated by Stella Rodway. London and New York: Penguin Books, 1981 [1960].

Wiley, Tatha. *Original Sin: Origins, Developments, Contemporary Meanings.* New York/Mahwah, N.J.: Paulist Press, 2002.

Wright, N. T. *Jesus and the Victory of God: Christian Origins and the Question of God.* Volume 2. London: SPCK, 1996.

—— *Evil and the Justice of God.* London: SPCK, 2006.

Young, Frances. 'Christology and Creation: Towards an Hermeneutic of Patristic Christology'. In T. Merrigan and J. Haers, eds. *The Myriad Christ: Plurality and the Quest for Unity in Contemporary Christology.* Leuven: Leuven University Press, 2000, 191–205.

Transcript

'David Quinn and Richard Dawkins Debate *The God Delusion* on *The Ryan Tubridy Show*', *The Irish Catholic* (Thursday, 4 January, 2007) 5–7.

Internet Sites Accessed

'Gaping Hole Found in Universe', Thursday, August 23, 2007, @ http:// www.reuters.com/article/newsOne/idUSN2329057520070823 (accessed on 21 November, 2007).

'Astronomers Find Enormous Hole in Universe', August 23, 2007, @ http://www.nrao.edu/pr/2007/coldspot/index.shtml (accessed on 21 November, 2007).

Eagleton, Terry. 'Lunging, Flailing, Mispunching'. *London Review of Books* (19 October, 2006). Accessed at http://www.lrb.co.uk/v28/ n20/eag101_.html 1–6 (19 July, 2008).

Index